A TREASURY
OF
OLD
SOULS

Other books by Eric Bergeson:

Down on the Farm
Still on the Farm
Off the Farm
Back on the Farm
Pirates on the Prairie

A TREASURY OF OLD SOULS

ERIC BERGESON

Country Scribe Publishing
4177 County Highway 1
Fertile, MN 56540
countryscribe.com

Cover and interior design by Annette Wood.
annettewoodgraphics.com

Cover photo by the author.

Printed in USA.

First Printing, 2015

ISBN 978-1-4951-6130-8

Acknowledgements

Many thanks to my encouragers and helpers: Tina Campbell, Gloria Kaste, Joe Sertich, Renee Rongen, Marie Seeger, Teresa Aakhus, Paul and Glenda Bergeson and Rolly Bergeson.

Thanks to the Bush Foundation, particularly Martha Lee and my fellows in the 2011 Bush Leadership program.

A special thanks to editor extraordinaire Carol Rehme, project manager Tracie Bergeson and book designer Annette Wood for their professional excellence and personal interest in this book.

Finally, thanks to Lance Thorn, my source of constant support.

Eric Bergeson

Foreword

Eric has had a love affair with the elderly since he was a young boy working at the Bergeson Nursery in Fertile, Minnesota. At the nursery, Eric was surrounded with people much older than himself, people he came to love and admire. It is Eric's love of the elderly that shines through every page of this book.

Eric brings a refreshing authenticity to his writing about his relationships with the elderly because his anecdotal reflections are the result of real life experiences and heartfelt affection. Eric is the real deal, and shows up in a t-shirt and a smile, approaching the elderly with ease, curiosity and respect. Eric sparks smiles on the faces of those around him, and holds his own on just about any conversational topic from sports to economics and history.

In *A Treasury of Old Souls,* Eric combines keen insight into what relationships are all about and how they enrich our lives beyond measure. He reminds us that the primary resource we bring to any friendship is our own being. After reading Treasury, you will come away not only with renewed appreciation of how love connects

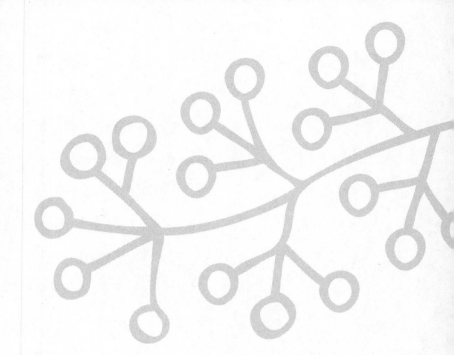

us with people of all ages, but an even deeper appreciation for the unique capacity for love and engagement in the hearts of the elderly.

Eric and I are cousins. We share a deeply held conviction that the human family is much larger than a blood connection. We believe it is important to befriend elderly people who are not our immediate relatives, expanding our definition of both family and community, enhancing our own life experience. Entering into inter-generational relationships brings a depth to life and a zest for living, reminding us that we can be fully alive until we die.

I commend and congratulate Eric for writing this important book, knowing it will entice a larger community to enter the lives of the elderly in a loving and meaningful way. As we read this book we learn of the many treasures the elderly bring to our lives, our communities, and our hearts.

The Reverend Dr. Kristina "Tina" Bergeson Campbell
Scottsdale, AZ

My Reasons

"I was scared of old people," said Fiona, a young Kiwi woman seated across from me on the ferry ride between the North and South Islands of New Zealand. "I had never known an old person in my life."

That changed. While riding the bus, Fiona saw an elderly man struggling to haul his shopping bags down the steps. She helped him to the street and let the bus leave without her.

"I could make it—if I only could find my cane," he said, apologetically. He had lost his cane the week before. Without it, he was almost helpless to get groceries and run other errands.

Fiona escorted him to his apartment where they visited. When she learned of other things he needed, she ran two small errands for him. His gratitude floored her. How many other people struggle like this on a daily basis? she wondered.

Eighteen months later, a private detective knocked on her door. "Is your name Fiona?"

Yes, she said.

"Did you help a man get groceries a while back?"

Yes, she said again.

The detective asked other questions to establish her identity. Then he delivered shocking news. The elderly man had died, leaving a small but significant estate. He named one recipient—the young woman who helped him haul his groceries when he had lost his cane. Knowing only her first name, he had described her as best he could. The estate's executors hired the detective to track down Fiona.

Funded by a fellowship from the Bush Foundation of St. Paul, Minnesota, I was in New Zealand to study eldercare. My partner Lance and I toured fifteen nursing homes. We talked with people who worked in every element of eldercare. We talked to a national nursing home inspector. We spoke with administrators of for-profit and nonprofit establishments. We visited nursing homes housing the big city rich as well as the rural poor. We met the chief lobbyist for the eldercare industry in New Zealand's capitol, Wellington.

Back in the States, I attended conferences dedicated to aging; a nursing home administrator convention; an Alzheimer's convention in Washington, D. C.; workshops on eldercare; and a conference on the crisis in eldercare funding. I visited dozens of nursing homes. I lobbied politicians on behalf of three separate organizations devoted to improving eldercare.

As a part of my Bush Fellowship, I helped organize the building of a much needed assisted living facility in my hometown of Fertile, Minnesota.

But nothing affected me like the conversation with Fiona.

As we contemplate an eldercare system we would want to live in ourselves, certainly we recognize that enlightened policies, adequate buildings, nutrition programs, education programs, and medical research must be addressed.

But what about human *connection*?

As I thought about Fiona's experience, I realized I had once been scared of old people, too. However, I had a distinct advantage.

In 1969, Grandpa phoned. He was ready to retire. It was time for Dad and Mom to take over the family business, Bergeson Nursery, founded by my grandparents during the Great Depression. My father Paul, a minister and instructor of biblical Greek in Winnipeg, Manitoba, and my mother Glenda, who tended my sister and I in the suburbs, made a fateful decision.

They accepted a higher calling.

We moved to the countryside eight miles from Fertile, an aging rural community in remote Northwestern Minnesota. I didn't know it yet, but we had moved into a different world.

All of our neighbors were near retirement. So were the employees at Bergeson Nursery, where I would grow up. Their children and grandchildren lived far away. Like many small towns, Fertile sent its young to the suburbs for work.

During my formative years, I watched these neighbors and friends age. I saw them go from full independence to nursing home care. I attended their funerals. Dozens of them.

Over those decades, I formed a connection with the older generation.

My parents set examples. They treated elderly neighbors and employees not as people deserving pity, not as irrelevant annoyances, but as significant human beings. Dad plowed snow from their drives. Mom chauffeured them to appointments and gave home permanents.

Soon after we moved to Fertile, old Oscar Erickson visited the nursery to buy a spruce tree. Oscar was so tight-fisted that, when he dipped snuff from his Copenhagen tin, he turned the other way to discourage someone who might ask for a pinch.

Dad showed him a potted spruce seedling, priced at $2.50.

"I'll be dead before that amounts to anything," Oscar groused. The two men laughed.

Dad pointed to a five-foot tall spruce, priced at $35. Too expensive. Oscar bought the seedling.

"You'll be dead before that amounts to anything," I chirped.

Nobody laughed.

Dad pulled me aside afterwards for a lesson. It is okay, he instructed, for old people to joke about their own death, but don't you dare bring it up yourself.

Oscar got the last laugh. He lived to be ninety-six. By that time, the tiny spruce had stretched into a stately thirty-foot specimen.

Slowly, I learned to get along with older people. It helped that we lived on the same farm as my grandparents. It helped that I worked at the nursery where most of the customers were retired. But even with so much exposure, I struggled to overcome my fears, my prejudices, my lack of understanding, my hesitancy to connect with people three times my age.

It wasn't until I met Fiona in faraway New Zealand that I realized my upbringing amongst older people was a boon. Circumstance allowed me to bond with seasoned seniors in greater numbers, in greater depth, than most people my age. So much so, in fact, I have come to view a connection with older people as spiritually essential, and I tap into it almost daily.

As my fellowship ended, I decided my contribution would not be buildings or policy. Rather, I wanted to tell the stories of the many elders who influenced and shaped my life.

This book is my attempt.

Eric Bergeson

Discovery

Grandma Olga

Olga Eleanora Johnson was born in 1903 in a log cabin on Minnesota's northwestern prairie. Soon after her birth, her parents, Ole and Emma Johnson, bought the 160-acre farm that remains in the family today and moved into a two-room log cabin on that farm.

Ole and Emma, who emigrated separately from Sweden to Minnesota, met and married in Norman County in their early forties. Olga, my grandmother, was their only child. Ole cleared the small farm—oak stump by oak stump—to plant crops. Emma churned butter at the Rindal Creamery three miles away. The little family attended St. John's Lutheran Church two miles to the west.

Both Ole and Emma were depressed; Ole drank and Emma was perpetually glum, leaving little Olga alone to do as she pleased. She talked to herself, collected imaginary friends, and devoted herself to schoolwork. She became the star student at the one-room schoolhouse perched on the corner of their farm. She developed flawless and beautiful penmanship. After eighth grade, she went off to high school in town eight miles away, boarded with townspeople, and wrote weekly letters in half Swedish and half English to her parents.

Olga developed deep friendships with her female classmates, both in Fertile and at normal school in St. Cloud, Minnesota, two hundred miles distant, where she received her teaching certificate in 1921. After teaching for a year, Olga went back to St. Cloud State University to get her degree. She wanted to be a professor.

As her second semester of schooling got underway, Olga received a letter from a neighbor back home. Your parents aren't well, the letter said. You must come home to take care of them.

Grandma's academic career ended that very day. She took the train home. When she stepped inside the door of the old farmhouse, she slammed her suitcase to the floor, her morale crushed.

"It was a bitter pill to swallow," she told me seventy-five years later.

While tending her parents, Olga shouldered a teaching job at the one-room school she had attended as a child. In 1926, she bought the first Model T in the neighborhood. She spent at least two summers working for extra money at a resort on Leech Lake where she was exposed to the drunken, wasteful, Roaring Twenties behavior of old-money vacationers from Chicago. It disgusted her, as did her father's drinking.

In response, Olga joined the local temperance lodge, which met in a large hall two miles west of her home. She rose fast through the ranks, and soon became head of the Minnesota and Wisconsin chapters of the International Order of Good Templars. Election to the position earned her a letter of congratulations from the mayor of Minneapolis, as well as recognition from other dignitaries.

A picture on the front page of the Duluth Tribune, circa 1931, shows Grandma in flapper gear as the newly elected head of the well-known organization. She was the first woman to lead the organization and the only woman in the picture. In the back row of the two dozen men who surrounded her—lesser officers and directors—stood Melvin Bergeson, a mere member of the board. They met and married. That convention was the last time Grandma would outshine Grandpa in her life. He made sure of that!

Olga and Melvin moved into the tiny log house with Olga's parents. Ownership of the farm was transferred to Olga in exchange for one dollar and "other valuable considerations." We now know that legal clause, in most cases, was understood to imply that you would care for your very old parents when they became unable to care for themselves.

Ole became incorrigible. He chased his new son-in-law, Melvin, around the farm with a pitchfork. Another time, Melvin ended up on the roof of the house while Ole wielded a butcher knife at the bottom of the ladder. As the winter of 1933 approached, Olga was pregnant with their first child and her mother was in decline. There was no way they could spend a long winter in the tiny house with Ole as crazy as he was. So Olga, Melvin, and Olga's elderly mother, Emma, moved twenty miles to the south to a shack called the Ramsey Place, next to Melvin's home farm. It was a long cold winter. They had no communication with Ole. They expected to find his corpse in the house come spring.

They didn't factor in the neighbors back home.

Ole wouldn't answer their knocks, but when the neighbors put hot food on the front step, the next morning they found the dishes empty and clean, ready for another meal. When Olga, Melvin, old Emma, and baby Edith returned in the spring, Ole was still alive but more insane than ever. He was taken to the county poor farm thirty miles away, housed with debtors, indigents, and the insane.

Olga's life grew more and more difficult. Her mother was in diapers. So were one or two of the six children Olga bore during the next ten years. And Melvin, busy realizing his dream of owning a nursery, was no help at all in household matters. Olga had at least two nervous breakdowns during those difficult years. Melvin's response was to hire a housekeeper and send Olga, via train, 250 miles away to a chiropractic retreat center in Canistota, South Dakota, a complex still in operation today. Decades later, Grandma described those weeks away from home as "the best weeks of my life."

Grandmother Emma sat in the corner and crocheted. She was involved with her grandchildren, perhaps, although they only remember her as dour and grumpy, probably the victim of several strokes.

And my grandmother Olga was worn out completely.

"Other valuable considerations," indeed.

Eric

My grandparents, Melvin and Olga Bergeson, started Bergeson Nursery in 1936 on a quarter section cleared of forest and rocks by my great-grandfather Ole Johnson. The business grew rapidly. By the mid-1950s, Bergeson Nursery employed a crew of thirty, sometimes as many as fifty, employees. In 1969, when Grandpa called Dad home to take over, the nursery's mailing list contained 5,500 addresses.

Over those years, life changed drastically on the prairie farms of Northwest Minnesota. Old-timers who painstakingly built up a 160-acre farm now found their land insufficient to support a family. Bigger machinery meant fewer people were needed to work the farms, which multiplied in size. The countryside, once brimming with hopeful immigrants and their massive families, drained of people. Returning World War II and Korean Conflict veterans moved to the coasts for work. Most graduates from small-town high schools went away to college and never returned.

By the 1960s, many of the older generation in our neighborhood had rented their land to large farmers. Some of them kept busy and supplemented their income by working at the nursery. Almost all of their children left long ago for the suburbs where they raised their own families. Therefore, when I arrived at the nursery as a five-year-old, I was surrounded by older people and only older people.

Although I made friends at kindergarten eight miles away in town, at the nursery I had one pool of people: older people who worked for Grandpa and older people who were his customers. I learned to make friends with people old enough to be my grandparents, hardy survivors of the Great Depression. My peers were Mildred, Elmer, Oscar, Inga, Ida, Ingvart, Selma, Alma, Art, Doris, Bernice, Olive, Carl, Henry, Hannah, and others with old-fashioned pre-World War I names.

One by one, each of the local old-timers retired. Yet they remained neighbors. Without their own children or grandchildren nearby, our family filled in. There were so few kids in the neighborhood that my sister and I actually received phone invitations to trick-or-treat at Halloween. One neighbor, Mabel Nelson, made delicious popcorn balls every year, a tradition that drew dozens of trick-or-treaters in the 1950s. But to get anybody to come knocking in the 1970s, she had to call around Halloween afternoon. Because kids were scarce, my sister, my new baby brother, and I were spoiled.

The old folks influenced my personality forever. Twenty-five years later, when I started a column in several area newspapers, readers who met me for the first time often said, "Is it your grandfather who writes the column?"

"No," I said. "It's me."

"Oh! I was sure it was somebody in their mid eighties!"

I took being mistaken for an eighty-five-year-old as a compliment. The mistake reflected my upbringing, however, and explained why I always felt a little out of sync with people my own age.

August

In Winnipeg, I hadn't known any old people. In Fertile, they were everywhere, and at first they scared me. Most of the men scowled. They smoked. They never smiled. They didn't even look at kids. And the old women were busy.

But when I climbed the big step into the school bus on my first day of kindergarten, I looked up—into the face of a gruff old man—and saw the warmest, most welcome smile I had ever seen.

August was a World War II veteran. He wore drab green work clothes. He smoked. And he took me under his wing.

While waiting for the kids to file out of school, August leaned against the chain link fence on the playground with the other tough bus drivers, as if they were still in the military biding time in some line. They glowered and pinched filterless cigarettes between thumb and forefinger.

But when I came around the corner from class, August leaned down, hands on his knees, and asked me about my day. The President of the United States couldn't have made me feel more honored.

My walk to the top of the driveway in the morning was a quarter of a mile and lined with distractions. One day after a six-inch snowfall, I only shuffled a few feet before I decided to make snow angels. When I didn't appear to get on the bus, August navigated our road and found me outside our trailer playing in the snow.

August was my angel.

Toward the end of first grade, a new driver took his place. The change filled me with anxiety. Where was August? Sick, we were told.

Later, I heard he had a stroke. What's a stroke? I asked. It is when something pops in your brain and you can no longer walk or talk, they said. Weird, I thought. Weird and sad.

Many days I sat in the bus, nose pressed against the window, thinking about August, wondering what he was doing.

Later, I overheard employees at Bergeson Nursery say August was in the hospital and when people visited his only response was a big tear rolling down his cheek.

Sometime during my second grade year, August died. But the adults used phrases like "passed away," and "it was actually a blessing," things I did not understand.

August's widow Nora was a peach. As I grew older, Nora always looked for me in the spring at Grandpa's nursery and gave me a hug. She told me how much August had liked me, and I told her how much I loved August, how he made me feel so much better those two years when I was the smallest kid on the bus.

I had many wonderful bus drivers, but nobody made me feel as safe and comforted as August.

Margaret Helm

My first memories of nursing homes weren't pleasant. A four-year-old in the late 1960s, I accompanied my father on a pastoral call to a woman who lost both legs to diabetes. Her room at the old folks home was glum, exposed pipes against the high ceiling painted the same grim green as the pimpled walls. I wondered how this poor woman could be happy in such an awful place. I never wanted to go back.

But two years later, Dad took me to a nursing home to see Henry Helm's wife Margaret, who suffered from Huntington's

Disease, an awful genetic condition which caused its victims to lose motor control and thrash uncontrollably. Dad, retired from the ministry to take over the nursery, brought a small New Testament along and read from it. No longer able to speak, Margaret grabbed at the Bible. Dad thought she wanted him to read more, which he did.

She seemed much calmer when we left, but the sight of Margaret thrashing stuck with me. I felt relief when the nursery crew returned to work after her funeral saying, "She looked so good."

Esther

Somebody had to wait on Esther. She stood like a fencepost in the middle of the perennials, with cat-eye glasses, tight mouth, fat cheeks, a tiny little body, arms limp at her side, hair in a mound of curlers held together by a scarf. Esther wanted help, but nobody wanted to help Esther. She was, according to the ladies in the office, a grouch. And, they added, she wouldn't buy any plants in the end, anyway. As the boss's cocky son, I felt entitled to help anyone I pleased. And I didn't like to see anybody go unserved. Although I knew very little about the perennials, I strolled over and said hello to Esther.

"Hi," she said in a grunt that came half through her nose. "What are these?" She used her cane to point at a group of potted plants.

"Silver mound," I said, reading the tag.

"Why are they so expensive," she snorted, in a statement more than a question.

"Because silver mound have magical powers," I said, aware the ladies were watching to see how I would handle this customer.

Esther was unfazed. "What kind of magical powers?"

"They'll fix what ails you," I said.

The edge of Esther's tight mouth rose a bit. "Find me something that's not magic," she said, still looking for a bargain.

Esther and I went round and round, me filling her full of baloney, she trying to hang me by my own petard.

In the end, as the ladies in the office had predicted, Esther didn't buy anything. She said she'd think about it. Esther's sister, who had given her a ride to the nursery, paid for her own flowers and the two got in their Dodge Dart and left.

The office employees said they were glad I helped Esther so they didn't have to. Esther used to be nice, they explained, but then she had a stroke and her personality changed. It bothered me some people avoided Esther merely because she wasn't the same as she had been.

Esther returned often with her kindly sister, who didn't seem to care that Esther's personality had changed. She always asked for me. She wanted to joust, so we jousted, back and forth, back and forth, until her sister finished picking out her plants and Esther had to leave.

"Your girlfriend came again," the staff teased when I missed Esther. "She asked for you!"

Several springs passed. I enjoyed seeing Esther at the nursery twice each season. After I reached high school, she invited me to stop by her place for coffee. I didn't have a driver's license yet and I didn't drink coffee, so I begged off. That became our running joke. I'll stop by when I can drive. And then I'll learn to drink coffee.

And I did. I was a senior in high school when I finally got my license. A couple of weeks later, I found the remote farmstead where Esther lived alone. I pulled into the yard and knocked.

Esther answered with her familiar lack of expression. After letting me in, she shuffled to the kitchen and struggled to get coffee ready. She didn't say much and stared blankly at me as I talked.

Sometimes she smiled slightly with the very corner of her mouth. We sat at her 1950s-style kitchen table. The silences were long but comfortable. I enjoyed Esther's bluntness. I loved how she plowed forward with everyday life despite her difficulty talking and walking. She still took care of her yard, which we toured. Her lawn was over an acre, much more than she should have been able to handle. She kept a large flower garden.

A month later, my phone rang.

"This is Esther," she said, in her monotone. "Come over."

Click.

I went over. Esther greeted me at the door. "Come here."

I followed as she shuffled toward the back rooms of her house.

Esther needed her mattress flipped. So, I flipped the mattress. That was the main mission. That was the reason she'd asked me to drive the twelve miles. But other important business remained. Coffee. Cookies. More time at the kitchen table, saying little, letting the coffee's steam fog our glasses.

Two months went by. Autumn came and the leaves fell. I took a drive past Esther's. Smoke billowed from her grove of oaks as I approached. When I pulled in, I found her in the middle of a massive pile of burning leaves trying to smother the fire, but the flames were out of control. I jumped out of the station wagon. I started stomping. Spotting a rusty fifty-gallon drum in the woods, I rolled it around to put out the blaze.

Esther was out of breath. She had a bad heart, she said. What was she doing burning leaves, I asked. I helped her inside, sat her down, turned on the coffeepot, and found the cookies as she huffed and puffed. She looked at me like I had saved her life. We had a good visit, although we didn't say much. She was too winded, and she popped a couple of tiny pills I recognized as nitroglycerin.

I went to college 300 miles away the next fall but drove home most weekends and cruised the countryside in our 1975 Dodge station wagon. Once or twice, I ended up out Esther's way and pulled in.

Every time I stopped at Esther's, she was in some sort of predicament. Once, I cracked the door open when she didn't answer my knock.

"Come in." Her voice sounded feeble.

Esther was in the bedroom, caught between a half-flipped mattress and the wall. I helped her finish the flip. Something about that mattress, it always needed to be flipped! How often, I never found out. But I helped more than once.

The next winter, Esther's nieces and nephews decided she must move to town to an apartment. She had no children, her husband had died thirty years before, and she shouldn't be by herself on the farm during the winter, they figured. She might fall on the ice and nobody would find her.

I visited Esther during Christmas break. She was proud of her new place and showed me every cranny, even the broom closet and the cupboard under the bathroom sink. Everything was in perfect order, down to the toilet bowl cleaner and Windex bottles lined in a row. We sat at the kitchen table and had coffee. And cookies. And we didn't say much.

In March, I came home for spring break. To pass time, I drove around town in the station wagon. It had been another white Minnesota winter. The snow banks along the streets rose above the car and blocked most of the parking lanes. I spun on the packed snow over to Esther's side of town. She lived in what we kids called the pig barns, long buildings that looked fitter for farm animals than senior citizens. I parked clumsily, halfway into the street, and crunched my way to the apartment building. After stomping snow off my boots in the entry, I listened outside Esther's door. There was noise inside, things being moved. What's she got herself into now, I wondered. I knocked.

To my surprise, a local named Dale answered the door.

"Is Esther here?" I said.

"She died two days ago," Dale said.

"Oh!" I said. "Sorry to bother you."

After a little hemming and hawing, I left. I knew Dale, but it took me a while to figure out why he was rummaging through Esther's apartment: He was Esther's niece's husband. My appearance at her door after her death must have struck him as just plain weird. I am sure he had no idea why I came knocking; nobody knew Esther and I were friends.

I contemplated staying home until Tuesday for the funeral, but the thought made me queasy. Only nineteen, I was exempt from the small-town expectation that you attend every funeral. In fact, the opposite was the case. People at her church would probably wonder what the heck a college kid like me was doing there. Looking for a free meal of hotdish and jello, perhaps?

I drove back to the Twin Cities to college, recalling quiet times at her kitchen table. I was glad I was there to put out her fire, to sit—reeking of smoke—after our brush with disaster, smiling over how appalled her relatives would be if they knew what she had been up to.

Esther and I had a connection. I value it to this day.

Play

Hannah Chalmers

My early connections with older people developed when I discovered that, no matter how crabby they looked, they longed for some lightheartedness. Middle-aged people, people the age of my parents and my uncles and aunts, mind-numbingly somber people in the prime of life, didn't have a gift for play. They were serious. Serious about work and serious about recreation. Serious about keeping up with the neighbors. Serious about producing normal children.

As a child at Bergeson Nursery, I discovered if I wanted to have fun I had best not bother the busy. Instead, I picked out those who had begun to shed their responsibilities, those in their sixties who had sold their cows, rented out their land, enrolled for Social Security, and worked only to "keep busy."

For a few years, I was a holy terror. Apparently, the son of the owner could get away with anything.

Gruff Miss Chalmers stayed at my grandparent's house for a few days each summer. To loosen her up a bit, I dubbed her Allis, as in Allis Chalmers, the tractor.

By way of explanation, I assured Hannah I only called her Allis because she was bigger than a tractor.

Grandma was appalled. "Show some respect for your elders!"

But Hannah loved the joke. We became friends and exchanged letters, even though I was only in the fourth grade.

Allis and I shared a love for rocks. One summer, a month after she departed, a big, heavy box arrived. It was a birthday gift for me. From Hannah.

It was a box of rocks.

Mrs. Rice

One of my favorite employees at Bergeson Nursery was Mrs. Rice, but I called her Mrs. Potatoes since we ate more of those than rice.

At morning break, Mrs. Rice opened a Coke. When she looked away, I slipped an earthworm into the bottle.

Mrs. Potatoes sipped her cold drink. And sipped. Nothing. No scream, no evidence of the worm. Eventually, she threw back the rest of the drink and slammed the bottle on the table.

"Ahhh!" She smacked her lips.

What? Had the worm dissolved?

Not long after, Mrs. Potatoes developed throat cancer. She died one year later. A naïve second grader, I was convinced it was because of the worm. I didn't tell anybody because I didn't want to go to jail.

Oscar

Cook Mildred prepared a daily noon spread for Bergeson employees. About twenty minutes before twelve, she set a platter of juicy tomatoes on the table.

She put it out too early.

Jalapeno peppers were also ripe, ready—and red. While Mildred puttered over the stove, I diced one and stuffed pieces into the center of a tomato slice.

The employees filed in and took their seats. I waited to see who would take the loaded tomato.

Oops. Aristocratic Oscar—so dignified, so proper, so kind—plopped it on his plate. I knew, even at my young age, that practical jokes weren't in his repertoire.

Oscar slid the whole slice of tomato into his mouth. He stopped short. Ever the gentleman, he discretely wiped the burning bits into his napkin before gravely announcing, "I think there may be something funny with the tomatoes!"

Bernice Schon

As I stretched my arms around a springy bundle of trees to find the other end of the twine, the phone rang in the cellar. I let go. The bundle sprang open.

"Ith thith Bergethon Nurthery?" said a childish voice.

"Yes," I said, trying not to imitate the exaggerated lisp on the other end of the line.

"I ordered fifty Chinethe puthy willow. Where are they?"

We didn't have Chinese pussy willow. I didn't even know whether there was such a tree.

"You promithed me fifty puthy willow!" she claimed, getting more worked up by the second.

I almost hung up.

Then her voice changed. "This is Bernice!"

I had forgotten. It was April Fools' Day. Bernice had tricked me for most all the years of my life. When she worked at the nursery, she convinced me that I had a wart on my nose. That my sandwich was moldy. That I was bleeding from my ear. At age eighty-four, she was still playing pranks and I wanted revenge.

I waited a year after the pussy willow incident.

Never married, Bernice was the Sunday School Superintendent at the Lutheran church down the road and had been for half a century. The church kids were *her* kids.

I used a heavy southern preacher accent when I called her a year later. "Hello, Miss Schon?"

"Yes?"

"This is Billy Joe Wilmington from the Committee to Convert the Lutherans. I was wondering if you would consider a love offering of five, ten, or twenty thousand dollars to help us steer Lutherans away from the path of destruction."

Silence.

Eventually, I had to fess up. I told her who I was. She acted hurt that I would want to convert Lutherans. The Lutherans! Who didn't *need* converting. She didn't get the joke. Yikes.

Sometimes, payback didn't work. But until Bernice died at the age of ninety-six, we kept up our pranks. We were both in on the jokes.

Usually.

Grandma Geiszler

While visiting a cousin and his family years ago, I rode in the back seat of the mini-van and entertained their five-year-old. It was going to get cold that night the radio announced and issued a "pet warning." In other words, better keep puppy inside or poor puppy might get cold. In obvious jest, I said I sure hoped they wouldn't put out a hippopotamus warning.

"Why not?" Jeremy asked, his eyes wide.

"Well, we'd all have to find room somewhere inside for our hippopotamuses!"

"Where could we put our hippopotamuses?" Without waiting for my answer, he listed the rooms of the house that were too small.

It wasn't long before Jeremy's humorless mother could stand no more of such foolishness.

"Jeremy, Eric is kidding," she scolded impatiently.

Suddenly, I couldn't wait to end my visit. What a killjoy!

My grandma Geiszler, who passed away when I was in third grade, put no such limits on imagination. A wonderful baker and cook, Grandma Geiszler specialized in a German coffee cake, kuchen, pronounced *coogan*. It was a running joke between us that not only was there peach kuchen and apple kuchen and cheese kuchen, but you could make kuchen out of *anything*.

I looked around the kitchen through five-year-old eyes. "Can you make kuchen out of … peas?" Yes, of course, Grandma said, you can make pea kuchen.

Can you make cabbage kuchen? How about hamburger kuchen? Grandma always said yes, and elaborated on how she might do it.

Never did she pause to make sure I knew she was kidding. The joke ran for years.

I suspect if one of her own daughters had tried the same trick fifty years earlier, Grandma might have grabbed her by the scruff of the neck and thrown her out the back door to play in the yard so she wouldn't be in the way.

Carl Erickson

At the nursing home where Grandma Bergeson spent her last years, old Carl Erickson moved in down the hall. Sixty years earlier, Carl and Grandma had danced together down at the Temperance Lodge. When Grandpa was alive, Grandma knew better than to mention her dancing past because he was not only opposed to dancing (the vertical expression of horizontal passion), but was furiously jealous of Grandma's earlier friends—to say nothing of dancing partners.

After Grandpa died, Carl visited Grandma when I happened to be there. Her eyes lit up.

"Well, if it isn't Carl Erickson himself. How are things down at the lodge?"

By this time the Temperance Lodge was long closed, but Carl, a man of few words, said "Fine!" and the two had some good laughs.

I was shocked to see Grandma's sudden display of a sense of play.

As her memory faded, her sense of humor grew. A woman who was once almost foreboding in her dignity and scholarly approach to life became a warm person who loved to hold hands and have her hair lightly stroked by her visitors.

Perspective

Great Aunt Olive

My great aunt Olive, born in 1911, has seen times both good and bad—but mostly bad. To my surprise, she recalls the Great Depression on the farm in Northwest Minnesota with great fondness. It was the best time of her life, she claims.

Aunt Olive's family was dirt poor. Her father suddenly passed away just as drought and grasshoppers descended on the family farm, leaving his widow Lena alone to raise seven children under the age of fifteen. The oldest, both boys, did the farming. Mama and the girls did the cooking and took care of the two baby boys.

The family survived, but they didn't do it alone. Neighbors and friends helped. All were in the same leaky boat. They shared farm tasks and machinery. Old Mrs. Hembre spun wool and made clothing for the children. The communal threshing of wheat was a neighborhood festival. The children were everybody's to care for.

Youngsters stayed overnight at neighboring farms without asking their parents, yet nobody reported them missing.

Aunt Olive's older brother, my grandfather Melvin, was twelve when his father died. A few weeks later, township authorities called on the families of the neighborhood to contribute to the building of a road. Grandpa hooked a team of horses to a scraper and did his family's part. A tattered picture of the event shows Grandpa in knickers (which, in those days, boys wore until they were confirmed in the Lutheran faith) and bare feet next to a dozen fully shod, burly men. The date is 1920. The now-abandoned road the men built through a deep ravine stands as an unmarked memorial to a time when cooperation between neighbors was an unquestioned and necessary part of daily life.

Another crucial ingredient to the happiness Aunt Olive remembers during hard times: There was always plenty of food. Fresh eggs, newly-butchered chickens, potatoes, carrots and onions from the cellar, fresh-baked bread, apple pie, strawberries—fresh or canned. Nobody had much money, but nobody went hungry.

Just as importantly, much of the family's day was spent growing and raising food. The link between work in the field and food on the plate was obvious. Families were directly rewarded for their hard work. And after a sumptuous supper, they played cards by candlelight until bedtime.

Aunt Olive and her neighbors enjoyed those times so much because of the solid human connection. Their togetherness wasn't the obligatory affiliation of a workplace, or the temporary bond experienced during a natural disaster, or the sometimes-begrudging alliance experienced by modern nuclear families isolated in their large suburban homes. No, the happiness Aunt Olive remembers arose from a steady, constant need to cooperate with extended family, friends, and neighbors to survive. It was a connection fostered by mundane daily tasks. It was a connection of shared circumstances difficult enough to keep people working together but not so dif-ficult that relations began to fray. It was a connection of shared dreams. New roads, new schools, new churches, dances, programs, parties, clubs, lodges, garden clubs, all manner of improvement associations sprang up like corn on the prairie after a June rain.

"Back in those days, you just sat the old people in a chair against the wall in the morning and expected them to stay there all day!" Aunt Olive says, obviously glad that at 102-years-of-age she wasn't shunted aside in the same way.

"Old Mrs. Larson always sat in her chair and we didn't pay much attention to her. One day, she just disappeared. The Larsons put out an emergency call on the party line, and all the neighbors gathered to search. It wasn't long before somebody found her inside a shock of corn, singing softly to herself."

Aunt Olive paused.

"I was envious of her. That's what *I* wanted to do, just run and hide in a shock of corn and sing to myself."

Kae Bergeson

After a brief Internet courtship and two visits to Thailand, my brother Joe brought his beautiful bride Kae home to Minnesota. Not at all what the family expected, Kae was no shy, retiring, Asian mail-order bride. She took root quickly. Soon, she had the rest of us gathering in her overflowing kitchen at mealtimes like a Thai clan.

When Dad shoveled down his food and edged toward the side door to putter in the shop, Kae grabbed him by the shoulders and sat him back down.

"In Thailand, old people *enjoy* their family!"

Before she arrived, Kae questioned Joe and learned that our parents were in their mid-seventies. That bit of trivia stuck in her head. When Kae arrived, she immediately began attending to Mom and Dad as if they were very old, not just ... old. She went to their house and cleaned, washed dishes, and brought food.

Well! Mom and Dad were still fully active and proud of it. It took a few weeks before they got across to Kae that they were more than able to wash their own dishes. Kae arrived at the nursery with the noble Asian view that the young take care of the old and are honored to do it. Mom and Dad appreciated Kae's respect but wanted to maintain their independence.

A bittersweet story Kae told illustrated the stark difference between the Asian view of old age and our view in the West. In Thailand, Kae's thirteen-year-old son (from her first marriage) had leukemia. After six years of fighting the disease, the doctors said there was nothing more they could do.

Kae asked her son, "Are you afraid to die?"

"No," he responded. "I am just sad that I will never get to take care of you when you are old."

Traditional Thais love, respect, and venerate their aged to an extent we can't imagine here. By comparison, few Westerners inculcate their youth with such traditional values.

However, after six months of living in the United States, Kae had a different observation.

"It is good that old people in America still work and keep busy," she said. "In Thailand, once they turn sixty years old, people sit around and moan and groan and wait to be served!"

Gloria

My friend Gloria recently retired from a forty-year career in elder-care, first as an aide, then as a nurse, and finally as an administrator.

"Care has improved dramatically," she said, before citing several examples.

According to Gloria, one of the biggest improvements came in the mid-1980s when routine catheterization of incontinent residents was replaced with incontinence pads.

"I'll never forget the day a truck dropped off box after box of Depends. By that evening, all the catheters were gone."

In one fell swoop, residents were more comfortable and mobile. Eventually, bladder infections, a bane of old age, were dramatically reduced. It changed their lives.

"We used to restrain people with dementia. I remember crawling under the bed like I was changing oil on a car, trying to get the restraints attached. Finally, we just quit!" She shook her head amazed such a barbaric practice had gone on so long.

Dogs, cats, carpet, adjustable meal times, rooms large enough to accommodate furniture brought from home, all reflect a new philosophy: A long-term care facility is a *home,* not an institution.

Grandma Olga

Grandma Bergeson was a dignified woman. She carried herself with pride. She spoke carefully, often with eyes firmly shut, and always in proper English. Her handwriting was impeccably beautiful, if stern. Although she and Grandpa never had money, she was blessed with the confidence that education, as well as independence of mind and action, can bestow.

Her dignified bearing lasted well into old age. However, as Grandpa and Grandma began to alternate a series of health problems—from heart attacks, strokes and broken bones, to smaller, nagging issues such as hearing aids, constipation, hemorrhoids, ingrown toenails, and other indignities (so called for good reason)—her confidence began to erode. So did the primness of her bearing and appearance.

Grandma's glasses were crooked, so Mom took her in for new ones. Grandma preferred the old ones. The new glasses disappeared.

The aunts bought Grandma a winter coat almost every year, but Grandma refused to wear them, insisting her zebra-striped fur coat, the only gaudy thing she ever owned, was fine despite the moth holes. The new coats were returned.

Some of the indignities were harmless. Others caused trouble.

Grandma started to hear demons. They screeched in the dark. The screeching brought back nightmares of the long winter nights she spent in that same house eighty years before, when her father was mentally unstable and possibly dangerous.

So, what do you do when Grandma hears demons? There wasn't a prescription for demons. Consulting a psychologist was out of the question. Grandpa was his own minister, so they had no reverend to perform an exorcism.

Grandpa ignored Grandma's demon issue, but Dad listened carefully to his mom and figured out the problem: The batteries of the smoke alarms in the bedroom and living room were low and squawked every few minutes. Grandpa couldn't hear that frequency, but Grandma could. By simply replacing the batteries, Dad cast the demons out of the house. Dad explained the problem to Grandpa—who immediately went to town and bought a lifetime supply of 9-volts.

No more demons!

But demonic shrieks weren't Grandma's only problems those long two years before she entered the nursing home. Her face was puffy, and the doctor couldn't determine why. She limped for years after breaking her leg in a fall. She no longer wanted company. She didn't want to cook much. The traditional Sunday afternoon lunch she had created for her family became a chore, and finally we assured her the long-standing ritual could end if she wanted it to.

Although she wasn't yet forgetful, we witnessed signs of decline. When she broke her leg, she was sure the doctors were "in it for the money" and that she really didn't need surgery to fix the brutal but clean break in both bones. Dad had to take a middle-of-the-night trip to the hospital to talk her into agreeing to the surgery scheduled at six the next morning. Grandma slowly healed at home, using a chair on casters to roll around the kitchen and prepare meals.

As Christmas approached the next winter, Grandpa had a heart spell and ended up in the hospital thirty miles away. Grandma couldn't be home alone and went to stay with her daughter Edith. I drove up to Ede's with their mail one evening and handed Grandma a stack of Christmas cards. She leafed through them, pulled out one particular card, and muttered.

"Oh, you just keep out of it!" she spat at the card as she opened it.

"What's the matter, Grandma?" I asked.

"See what you think of *this!*" She handed the card to me.

The card had a simple greeting from Elaine, a woman Grandpa and Grandma met years before at Bible Camp.

"'Have a blessed Christmas! Love, Elaine,'" I read. "Sounds pretty straight-forward to me."

"He's had her on the string for years!" Grandma snorted, implying Grandpa and Elaine were carrying on an affair behind her back.

Aunt Ede protested. "Oh for goodness sakes, Grandpa's eighty-two years old! What could they possibly do together at that age?"

The reality was that Grandma's suspicions and paranoia, fueled by a little reality and a lot of imagination, overflowed for the first time. She no longer had the means to hide her anger. The three of us talked it through. Grandma finally conceded that Grandpa and Elaine probably didn't have an affair. However, over the years, Grandpa had many women friends he spent more time with than Grandma. Now, the hurt was coming out. And it was not a dignified thing to watch.

When Grandpa improved enough, the doctors admitted him to the nursing home. At the time, the cost was reasonable enough that Grandma was also admitted—although today's standards would dictate assisted living for them instead.

Leaving home confused Grandma. She worried, worried, worried about the old house. What was going to become of her canned goods? Was everybody getting fed? Little things became big things and some big things that had been repressed came out. Visits with Grandma were a trial. How could we get her to quit worrying and fussing?

Grandpa improved enough to drive his car. One day, he loaded Grandma and their belongings without asking permission or checking out and moved the two of them back to the old, leaky house.

Grandpa did the cooking, the first attempt at preparing food in his life. The fare was grim. Family members brought meals occasionally, but it was an uncomfortable time for everybody.

Six months later, an ambulance carried Grandma to the hospital. She was bleeding internally and not expected to live. After she received eight units of blood, the crisis passed.

That afternoon, I visited the intensive care unit. Stopping at the nurse's station for a report, I looked through the ICU window at Grandma.

She glowed!

Her crooked glasses sat on the cart. Her hair, always in a bun, was down, combed. Long, silver, beautiful. Her cheeks shone pink. Her eyes twinkled. The swelling in her face was gone. I barely recognized her. Something about those eight units of blood gave Grandma an infusion of life.

As I walked in, she put down the book she was reading.

"And what do you have to say for yourself?" she said, all business, but with a twinkle in her eye.

It became clear that, for the first time ever, she did not know exactly who I was. So I told her. She asked what I was doing with my life. I'm studying to be a teacher, I said. She smiled with approval, told me to get on with it, then announced we had visited enough and I should leave.

Wow. Grandma's dignity was back!

Grandma spent the next seven years in the nursing home. But during all seven of those years, she carried herself with the dignity I imagined she had before she met Grandpa. When she was the first person to own a Model T in our township. When she was a respected teacher. When she was the first woman to lead a two-state organization. When she was wearing her flapper gear in the 1920s.

Those who served Grandma in the nursing home allowed her to recoup some of the dignity she had lost when she gave up her teaching career for a life of caring for her elderly parents and a flock of children.

Overcoming
Barriers

Henry Helm

As my Grandpa Bergeson grew older, he loved to visit the old and infirm. He was not very sociable with neighbors when they were well, but when they got sick he was right there and had just the right thing to say. As I grew and entered junior high, Grandpa asked me to come along on his visits. I resisted. Hospitals and nursing homes nauseated me.

Neighbor Henry Helm was a skinny man, tough as leather, with a voice muffled from decades of smoking Salems. He wore soiled work clothes and a dirty hat. He walked in long strides— no time for foolishness or kids—and seldom smiled or laughed. Henry was hard work incarnate, his only pleasure fishing trips to Roy Lake.

Then Henry got sick enough to be hospitalized. Grandpa, who didn't speak to him much when Henry was well, decided we should visit the hospital. I dreaded the visit like I dreaded a funeral.

Henry was clean-shaven, wearing a gown, and emasculated. He was glad to see us, but I was anything but glad to see him, especially in that state.

My head spun. I slid into the bathroom, shut the heavy door with a loud click, and barely leaned over the toilet before vomiting. I did not have the flu. I was merely overcome by the sight of once-mighty Henry in a hospital bed.

It wasn't the last time I vomited during a visit to a hospital.

Horace

Horace wanted a blue spruce tree planted in his back yard, and he wanted me to plant it. Although our nursery sells spruce, we usually don't do the planting. But Horace was confined to a wheelchair, so I decided to take on the job.

I knocked. Horace yelled for me to come in. I opened the door, and there sat Horace in his wheelchair, beer in hand.

I started talking about the spruce. Where should we plant it?

Horace stopped the conversation with an irritated wave of his hand.

"Wait a minute," he said. "Let's get something straight here."

"Okay," I said, taken aback.

"I may be a cripple and I may be drunk," he said, pointing a finger at me, "but I am not deaf!"

Apparently, I had been talking to Horace extra loudly. And he didn't appreciate it.

I had made the common mistake of assuming that because an elderly person has one disability, he must have all the others as well. If he uses a cane, we raise our voices. If she can't hear, we rush to help when she starts to rise. I once was chided for talking extra loudly to a person who merely had a broken arm. I had no idea. How embarrassing.

Long confined to a wheelchair, Horace was attuned to his limitations. He was also well aware of his abilities, and he didn't want people shortchanging what he could do.

Great Aunt Olive

When Great Aunt Olive was ninety-six, she decided the one thing she wanted to do before she died was hear the frogs in the swamp sing in spring. Since my house is near a swamp, I offered to pick her up at the nursing home for an outing. I double checked to see that she was wearing her hearing aid.

When we arrived at my house, I shut off the pickup and rolled down the windows. The sound of the frogs was deafening. I was sure Aunt Olive could hear them. No such luck. Her good ear didn't pick up a single croak. The hearing aid must have been on the blink.

On a whim, I put the pickup in four-wheel-drive and drove on a narrow spit of land protruding into the swamp. The pickup grunted through the muck.

"My lands!" Aunt Olive said, softly laughing at the absurdity of it all.

We reached the end of the spit, so narrow we couldn't get out of the pickup without falling into the swamp. Eager to hear the frogs, Aunt Olive opened her door and put her foot down toward the soggy ground. Under Aunt Olive was nothing but air.

"Don't take another step!" I yelled.

Fortunately, she hung there while I inched around the pickup in time to catch her and press her back so she wouldn't roll into the swamp. We found a solid patch of ground and planted her there. I had her hold onto the fender for stability.

The frogs were even louder. But Aunt Olive still couldn't hear a thing.

Aunt Olive had been looking forward to hearing the frogs for over a year. Since we were this far, I determined we couldn't stop now. I rummaged on the floorboard until I found a manila folder that I formed into a cone and held to her ear. I froze, hoping it did the trick.

Aunt Olive's lips widened in a smile. She heard the frogs! To top it off, the trumpeter swans trumpeted from their nest in the middle of the swamp, and she heard them, too.

"Now I can die in peace!" Aunt Olive announced in triumph. I loaded her back into the pickup and backed gingerly down the spit.

Alice

Before my performance, I greeted residents in the common room of a nursing home about one hundred miles from Fertile. I tried to assess the abilities of each as I shook their hand, or looked in their eyes, or whatever it took to get their attention and say hello.

I came across a well-dressed lady who was spunky and outgoing, qualities that, amongst the grim Nordics of northern Minnesota, are more often than not a sign of dementia.

"I am a puppy!" she announced brightly as she grabbed my hand.

I jumped right into her world. "And a nice little puppy you are!" I patted her on the back, congratulating myself for so deftly honoring her reality.

"No, damn you!" she shot back. "I am Mrs. Ralph Puppe. My husband owned the Chrysler dealership on the edge of town!"

Oops. Big mistake. But when I recovered and congratulated her on her local prominence, all was instantly forgiven and forgotten. Mrs. Puppe's need for significance, once honored, overshadowed her indignation that I briefly thought she was a dog.

Bernice Johnson

Great Aunt Olive's roommate Bernice lost all her fingers on both hands to the belt of a grain auger forty years before she entered the nursing home. After making the decision not to wallow in self-pity, Bernice had re-learned all household tasks. She also continued to enjoy crafts. However, she had some limitations.

While I sat in Aunt Olive's wheelchair reading one day, a staffer came in with great fanfare and in a sing-song voice asked Aunt Olive if she wanted to come down to the activities room to string beads. Aunt Olive is not interested in such things and had an excuse, company. Poor Bernice, who was sound asleep, had no such excuse. The volunteer awakened her and gave her the same pitch.

Bernice was too tired to explain, so she just shook her head, "Not interested."

The volunteer mercifully left.

Seconds later, Bernice mumbled, "Humph." I looked at her. She pulled her stubs from under the blankets and held them up. "So, how I am supposed to string beads with these?"

I had long forgotten about Bernice's hands, so the humor of her being asked to string beads with no fingers hit me late. Rather than thrust her fingerless hands under the nose of the volunteer, Bernice had faked sleep. The three of us had a good laugh.

Grandpa Melvin

My grandfather loved to eat peanut butter right out of the jar. However, he preferred old-fashioned, organic, natural peanut butter complete with a layer of peanut oil on top. For that, we had to drive to a grocer twenty miles to the south.

Because it kept well, my mother bought him an entire case of the stuff for Christmas.

When Grandpa opened the gift, he acted like it was a lump of coal in his stocking. Yes, he loved peanut butter and, yes, it was the brand he preferred. But Mom had overlooked something important. Grandpa's monthly peanut butter crisis always required immediate action—necessitating a personal appearance.

Grandpa did not like to out-and-out ask people to visit. He needed a reason. Peanut butter created the reason.

Mom had reasoned that a case of peanut butter relieved Grandpa of the trouble of running out of his favorite foodstuff. Grandpa wasn't relieved at all. Now he would have to think up another excuse for people to visit, and that meant work!

Christina

Christina came to the local nursing home with a terrible reputation for meanness. Townspeople actually feared her. She scowled as she sat in her chair in the hall.

Ready for a challenge, I greeted her. She grumbled. I commented on a computer within our view and said, "Things aren't like they used to be!"

"Damn right they aren't," Christina grumbled. "Used to be so much better."

"What do you miss the most?" I asked.

"Horses," Christina said without hesitation. "I loved all the horses!"

Christina went on to talk about the old days before the automobile, an invention she hated. In fact, she never owned one. She preferred horses. They were beautiful, they were graceful, and they were much quieter than cars.

"There used to be three livery barns in town," she barked. "Do you even know what a goddamn livery is?"

I happened to know livery barns were where people kept their horses while they did errands around town.

It was the only conversation I ever had with the notorious Christina. She died shortly thereafter. I was happy I was able to connect with her simply by asking the question, "What do you miss the most?" about the old days.

Listening

My Dad and Uncle Bob

My father has a knack for making a visit to a very old person mutually productive. He prepares questions for those he visits, questions about the past, questions the person he visits is uniquely qualified to answer. Sometimes, the question dies for lack of interest, but most of the time he gets an earful. Then he asks intelligent, follow-up questions that show his authentic interest in the topic.

My uncle Bob, a minister, was gifted at getting older people to share feelings about their past. He had no compunction asking questions others might have feared were snoopy, and he was rewarded with the loyalty of hundreds of people who regarded him as a close friend because he listened. He realized that although rural culture encouraged silent stoicism, many people had bottled years and years of pain and suffering. As their minister, he gave them permission to express pain during their last days. They rewarded Uncle Bob with adoration and love. When his turn came too early and he was stricken with terminal cancer, Uncle Bob needed a full-time social secretary to keep at bay the hundreds of people who loved him.

Following the examples of Dad and Uncle Bob, I make friends with older people with almost no effort.

Knowing that local nursing home resident Mel spent years at a military base in the Aleutian Islands, I looked up the town online, found out a couple of facts, and posed a single, educated query: What is going on with the town right now?

"Well, that's an interesting question." Mel leaned forward, prepared to talk. "In fact, the town has fewer than ten people left. Since the Cold War ended, the base was abandoned." His eyes widened in amazement. "Abandoned right after they'd built a twenty-million-dollar hospital!"

"Abandoned!" he repeated, shaking his head at the waste. "And it just sits there. Empty."

Gundersons

Each spring, the Gundersons made a trip to Bergeson Nursery from their farm sixty-two miles across the prairie. In their late eighties and papery frail, the Gundersons spent all afternoon at the nursery and eventually hauled away an impossible number of plants—impossible, that is, for us to imagine them planting. But the Gundersons loved plants, particularly roses, and they knew every variety of fruit, rose, and perennial in Minnesota. They weren't just good customers, they were a treasure trove of information.

The problem was, the Gundersons always showed up on the busiest day of the year. And before they started to pick out their plants, they insisted somebody named Bergeson admire their stack of pictures from last year's garden.

When I glanced from the cash register to see the Gundersons ease from their car and struggle across the parking lot, I wanted to run and hide. If Mrs. Gunderson saw me, she would hold up the stack of pictures and say, "I'll wait until you have time!"

"Who's going to look at the Gunderson's pictures?" My brother, parents, and I whispered and grumbled to each other as we rushed around helping younger, more agile customers.

When I finally approached Mrs. Gunderson, my attention was elsewhere. I was constantly getting pulled away, or pulled myself away—to get the phone, to answer another question, to fill the coffee pot, anything. The month of May at the nursery was a zoo, and the last thing I wanted was to hear Mrs. Gunderson's observations about a particular rose, or to sit through Mr. Gunderson's lecture on the differences in pit size of the Pipestone and Waneta plums.

But the Gundersons viewed their annual trip as a special event. They had been coming every May for sixty-five consecutive seasons. The nursery was as compelling on their calendar as Lent.

For several years, I managed to foist the Gundersons onto my mother, who would sit at a table with them and leaf through the entire photo album. As the years went on, however, and it became obvious that I was now the boss, the Gundersons would not leave until I had reviewed the pictures, too.

Finally, I relented. The next time I looked across the yard and saw the Gundersons struggling toward the office, I called somebody to take my place at the till, walked out to greet them, brought them to a table, got them a cup of coffee and a donut, sat down next to them, and said, "Let's take a look at those pictures!" I expected to spend the next hour gushing over photographs.

To my surprise, the session lasted barely ten minutes. In that short time, I picked up hints about how our plants performed relative to each other. The Gundersons brought so many pictures it was an education just seeing how their plants grew under different conditions. Once I concentrated, our time together passed quickly.

What the Gundersons really coveted, I realized, was my full attention. When I gave them that, they respected my time and went through the pictures faster than I expected. I was soon back at the till and the Gundersons were off to the greenhouse to pick out the year's new roses.

Mrs. Nelson

The intercom buzzed in my office.

Mrs. Nelson, a long-time nemesis, had arrived with a dead geranium. She wanted the boss. No one else could replace her dead geranium, although all nursery employees were authorized to do so without question.

For once, instead of glaring at Mrs. Nelson and curtly telling her she could simply go out and get her new geranium and nobody would argue with her, I decided to fake cheerfulness, fake that I was glad to see her, fake that I was listening, and see what happened. I even faked sorrow over the geranium she had murdered.

Strange thing. After a few seconds of faking, I started to really listen, to enjoy seeing her, and to be glad I was visiting with her. Responding to my initially false interest, she warmed up, apologized for bothering me, and wished me well. Salved by the balm of my full attention, the dead geranium issue melted away and did not ruin either of our days.

I could only hope Mrs. Nelson wouldn't kill the second geranium as fast as she killed the first.

Strategies

Grandpa Melvin

Until he entered the nursing home, Grandpa dictated his daily routine down to the finest detail. Once he needed care, however, an institution managed his day. This made Grandpa cranky. After he checked in, he took months to regain the will to live. He refused to watch baseball, his favorite pastime. He gave up reading.

And then he started to adjust.

After six months, Grandpa began writing a weekly gardening column for the local newspaper. After a year, he added a monthly devotional newsletter he sent out to one-hundred old friends. Two years into his nursing home stay, he wrote a sixty-page gardening book, which he published and marketed to 1,200 buyers. During spring and summer, he supervised a complete re-landscaping of the nursing home grounds.

But between his late-in-life accomplishments were episodes when the loss of dignity was too much. During those times, he took out his frustrations on aides and nurses and, sometimes, his family. Most of all, he exhibited his need for control with his wife.

Grandma was bed-ridden and had no remaining short-term memory. Grandpa took it upon himself to "protect" her from the evil nurses. To that end, he smothered her with attention and waited on her hand and foot. Eventually, Grandpa "protected" Grandma from getting out of bed to do anything, even exercise.

For as long as anybody could remember, Grandma was the last to finish eating at the table. After serving the family, she sat down but ate little as she watched to make sure others had enough food. Then she cleaned the plates, eating leftovers from the kids. Sometimes it took Grandma more than forty-five minutes to finish her meal. Her life-long pattern of eating meals slowly continued in the nursing home even after her memory faded. She let her plate sit while she looked out the window. Staff let her linger in the dining hall until she finished.

In the ideal arrangement, Grandpa stayed in the room to eat while Grandma was taken to the dining hall. If she ate in the room, Grandpa took her plate ten minutes after it landed and finished her food, even if he had plenty on his own plate.

When he was too sick to go to the dining room, Grandpa wielded his illness with the same coercion he'd honed throughout his life—and the staff allowed Grandma to eat in their room.

Of course he ate her food.

Was he trying to starve Grandma to death? When staff decided Grandma must go back to the dining hall, Grandpa threw a fit.

His offspring tried to talk sense into him. Some arrived at the nursing home; others called from afar. They were rebuffed. I was away at college, so I was spared the controversy—for a time. I happened to come home the weekend everything came to a head.

The phone rang.

"This is Pat," said the head nurse.

My heart sank. It was like getting a call about a child—not from the teacher, but from the superintendent.

"Your grandmother has lost ten pounds since your grandpa forced her to eat in the room," she said flatly. "He won't let her finish her meals, and we are worried she will go into decline."

Grandma was going to have to eat in the dining hall no matter what. Pat asked the family to help break the news to Grandpa.

This was not a welcome task. When backed into a corner, Grandpa was prone to violent explosions. The phone lines buzzed. Who would do the deed? Aunts and uncles had used up their credibility. Grandpa had cut them off. Meanwhile, I had not been involved with the present crisis and hadn't been to visit Grandpa in a couple of weeks. It was up to Eric, they said.

Thanks a lot.

Grandma didn't have ten pounds to lose. Nurse Pat used those lost pounds as leverage. Either the family helped reverse the situation, or the family was complicit in Grandma's eventual demise.

On a dark November evening, I drove to the nursing home in a haze of dread. I plodded past residents I normally greeted in the hall. I had a cold. I was hoarse. The back of my neck burned with anxiety.

Grandpa was glad to see me. I sat down in a chair next to his recliner. I remembered pictures of Lyndon Johnson buttonholing congressmen into voting for his bills by sitting a little above them, elbows on his knees, hands clasped, eye-brows raised. I adopted the same pose. Using my raspy voice as an excuse, I dispensed with pleasantries and got right in his face.

"Pat called me," I said.

Grandpa perked up. Nurse Pat was his arch-nemesis.

"She asked me to talk to you."

Grandpa smirked. Ah, the powers-that-be were at their wits' end. He liked that.

"Grandma has lost ten pounds in the last three weeks," I said.

Grandpa looked shocked, dismayed even. He shook his head side-to-side, as he always did when absorbing tough news. He couldn't have been surprised, but he knew how he was supposed to respond. At this point, I was still on solidly factual ground but was about to venture off into baloney-land.

"I know you have nothing to do with Grandma eating less," I lied through my teeth. "But the chart shows that Grandma's weight loss started when she started to eat in the room with you." At least that much was true.

Grandpa bit his lip.

"If the state inspectors show up and see that the chart shows a definite pattern of weight loss and that the nurses did nothing in response, they're liable to shut this place down."

Grandpa shook his head again. An anti-government conservative, he didn't want to cause the communists who ran the state of Minnesota to crack down on Fair Meadow Nursing Home.

"So," I continued as if it was no big deal, "Grandma is going to have to eat in the dining hall starting tomorrow."

To my amazement, Grandpa just shrugged. He seemed to know he'd lost this round, but I wanted make sure nothing went awry.

"Now, I know you get heart pains if Grandma eats in the dining hall, so I am going to come in and eat lunch with you."

My real intention was to hold Grandpa in a straitjacket in the event he threw a temper tantrum as they rolled Grandma from the room.

I finished my speech and leaned back. I was exhausted and my voice was shot. I had improvised my line of argument on the fly and was anxious to see if it worked.

Grandpa's brows lifted.

"You should be a psychologist," he said and laughed. It may have been his first laughter in a while. He had been in an extended funk.

When I arrived the next day, Grandpa had completely accepted the new reality. In fact, he told me, you roll Grandma down to the

dining hall and eat with her so she won't be alone.

"I'll eat here," he said. "I'll be fine."

That's how it happened. I ate with Grandma. And Grandpa was fine. The Fair Meadow Nursing Home version of the Cuban Missile Crisis was resolved. Grandpa had backed down. As I drove back to my parents' home to report, I felt as triumphant as Nixon returning from China.

My reward? Nurse Pat wrote on Grandpa's chart: "If you have difficulty with Melvin, call Eric."

Thanks again.

Eric

In high school, I had a routine but major surgery. Coming out of anesthesia was a surreal mix of pain, vivid nightmares, and nauseating painkillers that altered my sense of time. After being carted from the recovery room back to a private room, I was left alone by medical staff. My only anchor in reality was my mother, who sat quietly in the corner reading a book, a comforting and familiar presence when I opened my eyes between bad dreams.

Similarly, during long winter evenings spent at my grandparents' old house, we often had little to say. Grandma crocheted. Grandpa read the paper. We exchanged newspaper sections as we finished them. After exhausting the paper, Grandpa picked up a book. I picked up a baseball magazine I had probably read forty times.

I often went home feeling guilty we didn't talk more. Was I just using Grandma and Grandpa for their publications? After all, when I walked in, Grandma would simply point me to the paper or hand it over if she was reading it and say, "Grandpa's in the front room."

Shouldn't I have spent more time talking with Grandma?

Once Grandpa and Grandma entered the nursing home, my visits were often rushed, at least during the temperate months when

I was eager to get back outside. But when winter came, I didn't have much do so I sometimes pulled a book off Grandpa's shelf, sat in Grandma's wheelchair, and read for an hour while both Grandma and Grandpa did the same.

Great Aunt Olive, at 102-years-old, was usually ready to visit and tell stories at length. Not always, however. One time I arrived at the nursing home at an unusual hour. We fumbled for something to say. Nothing came.

"The vibes just aren't right," Aunt Olive declared, a hippy before her time. She suggested I come back another day.

The next time the vibes weren't right, instead of leaving, I pulled a family history book off the shelf and read silently. Aunt Olive stared at nothing, like I suspected she did much of the time when alone. I read for an hour, briefly discussed some discoveries with her, and left. By now, I had learned not to feel guilty or incomplete for not speaking much. The opportunity to sit together in silence was a treat for both of us.

93-Year-Old

In a nursing home in a neighboring town, a ninety-three-year-old woman was clearly entering her last hours of life. Staff called the family. A daughter who lived nearby was the first to arrive. Alone with her dying mother, she struggled to find something to say.

"Well, you've had a good life," she said.

Her dying mother opened her eyes and pointed to the corner.

"See that chair over there?" the mother rasped, barely audible.

"Yes?" the daughter replied.

"Go sit in it and shut up," said the mother.

The elderly woman drove home a great truth in dealing with the old, the sick, and the dying: There is no pressing need to talk. There is no need to sum up a life, to express every unexpressed thought,

to try to ease the situation by uttering platitudes. Sometimes, and more often than we think, the best thing to do is just sit.

Kiwis

Once, when I was exploring nursing homes in New Zealand in an effort to understand the eldercare system of another Western country, I stopped to ask directions at a museum in a small town. The ladies at the desk were curious about my mission and eager to talk. I asked them about the merits of small-town nursing homes versus large city facilities where medical care might be superior.

"At least in a small town," one woman piped up, "They'll sit with you if yore a-dyin'!"

Grandpa Melvin

The nursing home called. Grandpa had been taken to the emergency room with congestive heart failure. When Dad and I arrived, the doctor told us Grandpa wouldn't last more than an hour. As his lungs filled with fluid, his heart raced and he struggled to breathe. Too young to know any better, I felt the need to say—something.

"I love you, Grandpa!" I blurted from the foot of the gurney.

Well! My breach of Scandinavian stoicism did not pass notice, even by an eighty-something man heaving his last breaths. Grandpa opened his eyes and glared at me. The message seemed to be, "Just where do you think I am going?"

Within an hour, Grandpa came around and was giving me orders as though nothing had happened. Bring up some peanut butter. Find me a notebook. Make sure to bring the mail. That's how you show love to an old Norwegian man. You don't tell him you love him, you just do what he says. Now.

There is wisdom to sitting in silence.

Motives
and Drives

Eric

When I attended Bible Camp during my junior high years, an evangelist told a story designed to make sinful kids feel awful and accept the Lord on the spot.

An old lady lived alone, he told us. Nobody ever visited her. Nobody cared, he claimed, even though she lived in a neighborhood full of families with children. She was discovered dead in her chair, her diary on her lap. Her last thirty days on earth, she had written the same sentence on each page, "Nobody called today."

Tears flooded our eyes. How awful those neighborhood children were for not visiting the elderly and infirm. The evangelist pleaded with us to find time to visit one old person. To give them a call.

Guilt is a horrible motivator. No one wants to think there are forsaken, dependent people waiting for a visit, scribbling in their diaries, "Nobody called today." When faced with such sadness, we tend to look the other way.

However, the preacher's message stuck. I couldn't get that woman and her diary out of my head. I vowed to keep my eye open for the lonely elderly and, at the very least, step out of my way to say hello.

But charity visits, I learned, create a tidal wave of uncertainty. Will one stop be enough? Once started, must the visits and the relationships continue? Will I feel burdened? Will I be overwhelmed by expectations?

I mean, stop in once, and you risk being called every time she needs her mattress flipped. What a slippery slope!

And, if I stop visiting?

Certainly, the preacher's guilt-laden story served a purpose. But he failed to follow through, to mention the loving and lasting rewards of forming relationships with the aged.

Although a fine dose of guilt first motivated me to reach out to those I didn't know, only years later did deeper, more solid motives develop: Old people are fascinating; each has a story to tell; and visits often benefit me as much or more than the recipients.

Great Grandma Lena

As she approached sixty, my great-grandmother Lena Bergeson, known to family as Mama, moved from the farm into a little house in town and eventually, after a stroke, became one of the first residents in the brand new nursing home built in the mid-1960s.

Early on, long-term care facilities in rural Minnesota weren't managed by trained professionals. Retired Lutheran ministers ran most of them and a lot of those ministers, including the one at Mama's home, had no idea what they were doing. This particular nursing home was administered by a man who figured the place should be run like a reform school.

Mama was known for her kindness and even keel. But when the administrator tried to limit the possessions she brought to mere clothing, she rebelled, a pioneering advocate for resident rights.

Mama didn't just confront the administrator. So respected and connected was she in town that when she gave the word, the administrator was fired. She brought her belongings into the nursing home as she wished.

But according to Mama's daughter, Aunt Olive, there was one thing Mama didn't get.

"Nobody ever took her for drives," she said with regret. "We never even thought about it."

Aunt Olive remembers how excited Mama was when somebody took her forty miles to a funeral, one of the few times Mama left town during her entire retirement. Back then nursing homes didn't have a bus. The thought of taking the residents for a drive didn't occur to most families, and it hadn't yet occurred to those who ran the nursing homes.

Great Aunt Olive

Great Aunt Olive has loved going on drives all her life. When she still had her license, she took long jaunts in the countryside with her girlfriends. After she gave up her car, her friend Florence picked her up and the eighty-seven-year-olds headed east into the big woods of Central Minnesota, picnic baskets in tow.

Since entering the nursing home, Aunt Olive seldom misses a bus ride. Regardless of the effort it takes to load them, the activities department recognizes the joy residents derive from a weekly outing. Sometimes they drive fifty miles to Walmart, or they take a spin around town or into the country to see how the crops look.

Aunt Olive thinks those trips are the best part of being in the nursing home. When she found out the bus was donated, she penned a letter of thanks to the anonymous benefactor. She wrote about seeing the lilac blooms in spring, the clover blooms in summer, the old fences, the Amish and their plough horses, the combines harvesting wheat, the mountainous thunderheads in summer—all things the bus rides allowed her to see. She thanked the person who donated the van for "expanding the world" of people confined to a nursing home. After several revisions, her letter was complete.

The nursing home administrator, who hadn't spoken with the anonymous donor for six years, transmitted the letter. Two days later, the donor called the administrator.

"It is time for a new bus," the donor said. "How much will it cost?" Within weeks, a $60,000 bus was on order. Aunt Olive's letter appeared in the local newspaper along with the announcement of the new coach. She was given full credit for inspiring the donation. The updated bus became one of many highlights of her old age.

Mr. Janicek

One perfect September afternoon, old man Janicek sat on the bench outside the nursing home. Tears ran down his face.

"Would somebody *please* take me to Rollag?" He gripped his cane with both hands.

It was Labor Day weekend, and the Rollag Steam Thresher Reunion was in full swing. The world's largest collection of antique tractors, steamers and machinery was cranked up fifty miles to the south, belching smoke.

I felt so bad for old man Janicek I almost loaded him in my car. But his daughter came along and took him inside.

"You know your heart can't take a trip like that," she scolded.

And that was that.

Old man Janicek died a few weeks later. In a bed with the restraining bars raised and no family near. Of a heart attack.

I can't help but wonder whether he would've died happier at Rollag amid the relics of his youth.

Eric

During our summer vacations, Dad bought stacks of postcards and sent them to all of our elderly neighbors, even those he didn't know well. Those postcards, as small a gesture as they were, won Dad an amazing amount of appreciation from people who seldom traveled themselves. They seemed to never forget it.

Taking a cue from him, I tried the same trick.

Before I left for a trip, I made a copy of the local nursing home directory so I wouldn't forget the names of the people I knew there, which was pretty much everybody. During a break in my travels, I bought a stack of fifty postcards and wrote a short message on each one, personalizing it if I could, using a generic greeting otherwise.

Never has one little gesture earned me so much friendship—and not just with the old people. Turns out, they showed these remembrances to relatives. Friends. Staff. And showed them repeatedly.

It has been years since I pulled that shameless ploy. Most of the recipients of the cards have long since died, but occasionally a surviving relative approaches me with heartfelt gratitude.

"Emil really enjoyed that card you sent him from Arizona."

Written communication on real paper is never passé with the elderly, I've discovered. It is personal. It shows caring. And it can be read and enjoyed over and over.

Great Aunt Olive

Two weeks after her one-hundredth birthday, Great Aunt Olive decided it was time I took her on a long-discussed drive the 290 miles to her birthplace. After meeting with the staff of the nursing home to assess her possible needs during the drive, we set a date.

The day arrived cold and windy, but we set out anyway, picking up Cousin Monica along the way. For thirteen hours we traveled, stopping at the long defunct School for the Blind in Gary, South

Dakota, where Olive's aunts worked in 1910. We stopped at the farm where she was born in 1911. At the cemetery where her toddler sister was buried in 1907, four years before Aunt Olive was born. At the site of the church where my great aunt was confirmed. At the site of a one-room school, long since torn down, where Aunt Olive taught Danish kids for one year. Then we pressed on to the town where her brother had served as mayor, down the street he named Bergeson Drive, and then back north, arriving home at 9:00 p.m.

Cousin Monica and I alternated driving. Worn out, I took two naps in the back seat. All through the thirteen-hour drive, Aunt Olive's head never once touched the headrest. She wanted to be awake and alert the whole day. At a convenience store, we encountered a former friend of her brother's. She charmed people in restaurants.

Every moment thrilled her.

It was a drive to end all drives. And it was a complete success.

Old School

Corrine Hermanson

As second-graders, we watched the third grade teacher and dreaded our next year under her command. Corrine Hermanson never smiled. A tall stately woman, she cruised the corridor in long, slow strides. She wore bizarre glasses. She had a deep voice from decades of smoking. She scared us.

For the first few days of third grade, we cowered under Mrs. Hermanson's stern gaze. She didn't yell at us. She didn't do anything mean. But we knew to fear her, so we did. For crying out loud, our parents feared her, too. And Mrs. Hermanson did nothing to melt the ice between us. She used her reputation and our fear to give her a head start on the year. By the time we caught on that she was a deeply caring human being, she had us by the ear.

She could be rough. Her tobacco breath nearly knocked us over. Once my buddy and I came around the corner into the cloakroom when we weren't supposed to be there and caught her changing her panty hose. We ran off, scared she would have our hide, but the incident was never mentioned. Apparently, it was its own punishment.

Mrs. Hermanson brought me out of my shell. She gave me confidence. She challenged me. She laughed under her breath at my sometimes smart-aleck remarks. She gave me books to read at home. She suggested books out of the library. She winked at me with her face oh-so-somber.

I became Mrs. Hermanson's pet.

She moved me to a desk right by hers, where it became my job to pick up the used tissues she tossed toward the wastebasket—and missed. I liked her manner, her deadpan sense of humor. She didn't care if only half the class got it.

When we had our first parent-teacher conference, she insisted her students attend as well. No other teacher did that in those years. And my poor mother was shocked at the friendly, overly-familiar way I treated the great Mrs. Hermanson. By the end of the school year, I loved Mrs. Hermanson.

She retired a few years later. At our ten-year class reunion, she showed up where we were scheduled to take a picture. She was ninety. I bounced down the gym bleachers, along with my friend of the panty hose episode, to greet her.

Mrs. Hermanson wasn't so tall anymore.

She shook our hands formally. "Never retire," she said. "It stinks."

That was our last lesson from a favorite teacher. Two years later, her obituary appeared in the local paper.

David Bishop

In 1996, I spent a winter working as a page for the Minnesota House of Representatives. My fellow pages were recent graduates who hoped to climb the capitol ladder, starting on the lowest rung. I was there just to watch, knowing I would return to the nursery in March for another season of selling petunias and apple trees.

The first day of work at the Capitol, we were warned about Representative David Bishop (R) of Rochester. If he yells at you, we were told, don't worry, he yells at everybody. Don't take it personally. After all, he's old school.

When the Speaker of the House gaveled the opening session to order, there sat impressive Representative Bishop at a desk near the front. Well over six feet, he glowered at those around him. When things didn't go his way, he got cranky. Sometimes he stormed out. Sometimes he grabbed his microphone and scolded other representatives, even those of his own party. But when Representative Bishop rose to speak, the House chambers quieted. He was respected.

As the weeks went by, I was handed a plum job helping coordinate the high school page program, a new batch arriving each week. Although they worked on the House floor, sessions were often short, so the rest of the time the young pages listened to speakers. It was my job to round up the speakers.

I heard beneath his rough exterior Rep. Bishop had a soft spot for students. With some trepidation, I invited him to speak and he agreed. I advised the students that Rep. Bishop was old school, but they should not be intimidated and just enjoy him. He stormed into the conference room and roared. They loved him.

Dave Bishop was a brilliant man. A retired millionaire lawyer, he earned a graduate degree from Harvard at age sixty-two. He introduced complex legislation. He hired lawyers out of his own funds to travel the country and research the legislation he proposed.

He was respected by politicians on both sides of the aisle, even those who felt his wrath.

My best memory of Rep. Bishop happened during the prayer given by the day's chaplain during the opening of a House session. We all stood. I was up front near the page bench, facing the representatives. The prayer that day was more like a little sermon, so we didn't shut our eyes. It was clever. In the middle, the preacher inserted a scripture verse that directly rebuked the absurdities in the previous day's House debate. I understood the reference and couldn't help smiling. As I looked around the room, only one other person was smiling, and broadly: Rep. Bishop.

Our eyes met. We were in on the joke.

After that, the great Dave Bishop treated me like a long-lost friend. In fact, when my supervisor wanted me to return the next year to work the legislative session, he got down and dirty. He asked Rep. Dave Bishop to write a note to me. It read, "Get down here where you're supposed to be and get back to work!"

Rep. Bishop was dazzlingly intelligent and did not suffer fools gladly. He yelled at constituents who approached him with stupid requests. He intimidated members of his own party. He roared with indignation when House traditions were breached. But he was re- spected and treated with deference because everyone in the Capitol knew nobody worked harder crafting laws to improve the lives of the people of Minnesota than Dave Bishop. Because he never cared to lead his party, he remains relatively unknown outside political circles. But within those circles, he is a legend.

Bob

Bob was the consummate professional. A lawyer like Representative Bishop, Bob worked long hours on titles, wills, and city attorney business. He came home to his beautiful house down by the river and said little about his work to his wife Sharon and his four boys, one of whom was Roger, a high school buddy of mine.

Bob and Sharon were kind to Roger's friends. We often used their lake cabin to sail, swim, and canoe. Sharon was generous with snacks; Bob fired up the barbecue.

But Bob was old school. While we kids were busy being kids, he remained aloof, lost in his thoughts. I don't remember having a single conversation of any depth with Bob until I had graduated from college with a relatively impractical degree in history. Casting about for a career, I decided to go to law school. I did well enough on the entrance exam to be optimistic about my chances for acceptance. Application materials from universities piled up in the mailbox.

I needed letters of reference, including one from a practicing attorney. The only actual lawyer among my acquaintances was Bob, so I called his secretary Fran and made an appointment. Although I knew Bob, when the day came and the hour approached, I was as scared as if I was going to have a tooth pulled.

Bob seated me across the desk from him. After very little small talk—not enough to set me at ease—he asked the purpose of my visit.

"I am thinking of law school," I said. No change in his grim expression.

"I did well on the LSAT," I added, hoping for a glimmer of excitement. Nothing.

"Eric," Bob said, his office chair creaking backwards as he looked toward the ceiling, "I have one word for you."

"What's that?" I said with an uncomfortable laugh.

Known for his courtroom dramatics, he leaned forward, put an elbow on his desk, arched his furry eyebrows, and glared.

"Don't!"

Bob let his one word sink a bit before elaborating.

"You aren't cut out for it. You'll hate it. I know you well enough to know you will hate every minute of it."

He sat back and looked out the window.

"I know, because I hate it. I hate every minute I am writing wills and searching titles. It is a drag. It is not for you. You need more stimulation than that. I know you!"

Wow. It was a five-minute meeting. I didn't even get a chance to ask Bob for a letter of reference. But I knew he was right. I went home, stacked up all the law school applications, and threw them in the wood stove.

Despite Bob's boredom with his job, he didn't quit at retirement age. Instead, he retired from his practice in town and became a full-time public defender known for his full-throated defenses of the most obviously guilty clients. The poorer they were, the harder Bob worked to get them off. He spared no witnesses in his efforts, mocking their accounts, poking holes in their stories, demonstrating the weakness of the prosecutor's case.

"Bob never had a guilty client!" joked a judge years later.

When a cop testified that Bob's client had thrown full beer cans out the car window while driving and that he, the cop, could read the labels as the cans rolled down the road, Bob went to the liquor store and filled his brief case with a variety of beers. At trial, he rolled cans across the courtroom floor and demanded, "Tell me the brand of each."

Of course, the policeman couldn't.

The judge called Bob to the bench and chided, "You've got to quit this circus."

But Bob made his point and got his client off the hook.

Bob hit his stride at age seventy and had the most rewarding years of his career before finally calling it quits.

By now, I contemplated building a house. I spent an entire winter designing it for a perfect spot in the woods, by a swamp. It was time to either make a down payment or postpone the project until I could actually afford it. Roger, home from the Twin Cities, invited me to supper at his parents' house the night before my big decision. While Sharon prepared dinner and Bob paced, I sat in the living room with Roger, drinking beer and describing my dilemma.

All of a sudden, Bob came around the corner, eyes afire. He raised a bushy eyebrow, just as he had fifteen years earlier. This time, he pointed his bony finger at me and said, "Eric! Build... the...house!"

As he walked away, he added, "I didn't have the money when I built this house, either. But I've never regretted it. Best thing I ever did. Build the house! The payments look high now, but they'll shrink."

The next morning, I signed on the dotted line. And I have never regretted it. Bob was right again.

When Bob was eighty-two-years-old, he started to repeat himself. He thought his best friends were stealing his woodworking tools and lawn equipment. It was not a happy time. Nobody knew it yet, but he was in the early stages of Alzheimer's disease. As his memory faded, I reminded him about the two times he changed the direction of my life.

"Aw, bullshit," he grumbled. "Pure bullshit."

One of Bob's friends, a judge, was eventually named Chief Justice of the Minnesota Supreme Court. Roger, who lived in Minneapolis, wanted his folks to see the swearing-in ceremony but was not eager to have them drive themselves and asked if I could chauffeur them the 300 miles to St. Paul.

For the first time ever, Bob and I talked at length. He told me about his service during World War II, when his typing skills got him removed from a unit in Italy just before it was destroyed in battle. He told about his brief career in sales, his decision to go to law school, his years of boredom as a small-town lawyer, and his final triumph as a no-holds-barred defender of indigent clients.

A couple of times during the two days, I repeated my story of the two times he changed the course of my life.

"Bullshit," Bob mumbled. "Pure bullshit."

He was a professional. He was not given to small talk. He loved his courtroom work. Like many from the old school, he had a heart of gold. Drunk clients felt free to call him from jail at three in the morning. His gruff manner might have been off-putting to many younger people, but that was their loss.

Dr. Berryman

I attended a small religious college for one reason—the majestic, four-manual Allen organ dominating the stage of its beautiful chapel. When I enrolled, I imagined the music of Bach played daily as a prelude to Chapel and great Reformation hymns sung heartily by the student body of 1,200.

What a disappointment. The students weren't interested in Bach or the great hymns. They preferred insipid praise choruses sung in unison. More often than not, the massive organ console was hidden behind curtains.

In mid-October, I signed in to Chapel and walked the ramp into the auditorium. I couldn't believe my ears. Strains of Bach's delicious "Arioso" floated over the bustle. When I gained a view of the organ console, my dream was belatedly realized. There sat a gray-haired man, looking like God himself, lost in the music, oblivious to the gabbing students in the auditorium behind him.

The organist was Dr. Edward Berryman. During the service, he played the flashy toccata from Vidor's "Fifth Organ Symphony." Young undergraduates recognized his excellence and gave him a huge ovation. As a fan of pipe organ music since eighth grade, I was smitten.

Dr. Berryman came to campus only two days each week. I wanted badly to meet him, but didn't dare intrude on his teaching schedule. My opportunity came in the dining hall two weeks after his chapel performance. I saw him far up front, dressed to the nines, gray hair swept grandly back, selecting a carton of milk from the cooler as if he were drawing the knob of the thirty-two-foot stop on a mighty Aeolian-Skinner.

Organists are egotists, and Dr. Berryman was the supreme commander of every room he entered, even a cacophonous cafeteria. After I worked my way through the line, I found him holding court at a table nearly full of football players. He was making conversation as best you can with college football players when I sat down at the only open chair, a bit scared.

Dr. Berryman asked my name and hometown. After the formalities, I jumped in. "When are you going to entertain us in Chapel again?"

"Well, we'll try for edify," he said with a twinkle in his eye, playfully objecting to the title of mere entertainer. "Do you have any requests?"

I said yes, I would like to hear him play the "Fantasia and Fugue in G Minor" by Bach.

"Sure!" he said. "I will do that."

I assumed that would be the last I heard of it.

Several weeks passed before Dr. Berryman played in Chapel. When he did, he introduced the selection I had requested, an esoteric fifteen-minute piece that substantially ate into the time allotted to the morning speaker. I couldn't believe he remembered. I couldn't believe he elbowed his way into using Chapel time for a long Bach piece.

To top it off, when he bowed after his performance, he found me ten rows back in the full auditorium and gestured to me in a grand manner, as if he were tipping his cap.

For a freshman overwhelmed by the strangeness of college, it was an unforgettable moment. Within a year, I asked Dr. Berryman to teach me, even though I could not read a note of music. He agreed and worked hard with me, despite my inabilities. In two quarters of work, I memorized the gigantic "Toccata and Fugue in D Minor" and played it for a recital. Just before I left the college for good, I played the piece after Chapel. The students, who usually fled to the exits, stayed until I finished and gave me a thrilling ovation.

Dr. Berryman was dignity incarnate. The twinkle in his eyes warmed my heart. It took courage to approach him, but when I did, the rewards flowed.

Before Dr. Berryman died of Alzheimer's disease at eighty-eight, I paid a few visits to him in his suburban home. He still had the old school magic. He composed music until he could compose no more. He played organ even after he couldn't remember names. And he never lost his regal bearing.

Dr. Berryman has been one of the bright spots in my life.

Liturgies

Grandma Olga

You could set your clock by our mail carrier. He was as prompt as the school bus. The bus driver picked us up at 7:51 each morning, and the mailman dropped the mail off in the box at 1:19 in the afternoon.

At about 1:25, hot or cold, rain or shine, Grandma Bergeson—who had just dried the dishes from the noon meal—put on her duds and marched a quarter-mile to the mailbox.

Most days I was in school when the mail came, but in the summer, I was home and bored. The arrival of the mail was a big event for me, too, as it could include *Sporting News, Sports Illustrated, U.S. News and World Report,* or some other word from the outside world. As the hour approached, I sometimes stood by the mailbox, grabbed the bundle directly from the postman when he came, ran it down to Grandma's house, and took out the magazines or whatever was of interest to me.

I thought I was doing Grandma a nice favor by getting the mail, but I was not. The arrival of the mail was as important to Grandma as the arrival of the school bus to me and her daily opportunity to get fresh air, particularly in the winter. It was, in fact, her only chance to get fresh air—unless she was able to work in the greenhouse. Grandma raised a big family during the Great Depression. She was not one to waste anything, not even steps, on something as silly as a walk. By getting the mail before she had a chance to, I robbed her of an excuse to exercise. I disrupted her routine, and Grandma prized routine.

After supper in the winter, I crunched over packed snow to Grandma and Grandpa's house across the yard to pore over their newspaper. They subscribed to the daily; my parents did not. Grandpa and I discussed news items while Grandma puttered in the kitchen, putting away the supper dishes. Then Grandma moved to her living room chair and crocheted while Grandpa and I visited.

At 8:30, Grandma put away her skeins of yarn, struggled out of her chair and went to the kitchen to put together a snack for us. Hot chocolate or cider in winter. Nectar in summer. Crackers and cheese. Cookies as hard as golf balls. Herb tea. Open-faced cheese sandwiches. Grandma's spread was the signal that bedtime was approaching and Grandpa and I should start winding things down for the night.

As I grew older, I didn't always feel like staying for the entire ritual. I was tired of it. Waiting for Grandma to ready a snack made me impatient. I wasn't hungry. I had friends to phone. Maybe I wanted to bolt out the door at 7:30. But when I tried, Grandma jumped from her chair and frantically clanked dishes in the kitchen. I was not to violate the routine! Never mind that none of us really needed to eat another meal two hours after supper. The ritual of a snack before I said good night and went home had been established.

Sunday afternoon coffee was another of Grandma's ceremonies. In the springtime, the nursery was a zoo on Sundays as customers picked up plants on their day off. Grandma prepared snacks in her house for all the employees and family members. Everybody, *everybody*, rotated through Grandma's before she started cleanup. Sunday coffee continued into the winters when no employees were on hand and none of us was working or, for that matter, hungry for a mid-afternoon meal. No matter what, though, we were expected to show up at Grandma's at 3:00 Sunday.

Oh, how I resented glum Sunday afternoons. Anticipating the school week, I wanted to hide in my room and listen to the radio. But I dragged myself over to Grandma's and always enjoyed myself.

Grandma knew what she was doing. Later, I realized her ceremonies were her way of coping with the short, cold days and long winter evenings. As she aged, the customs she established gave structure and purpose to retirement. Grandma later told me that she, too, had had trouble with glum Sunday afternoons since her childhood. She cultivated a pattern with a purpose; preparing afternoon lunch gave Grandma's dreaded Sunday afternoons shape and expectation.

Eric

When things get busy at the till in the spring, I often get irritated at another habit common amongst older folks: The cash register ritual. Never does the Great Depression seem so recent as when it is time to pay the bill. While I ring up nursery purchases, checkbooks stay deep in purse or pocket, as though it's questionable whether money will be due or not. When the purchase is totaled and it is obvious that, yes, payment will be required, then and only then does the customer reluctantly reach for her checkbook. Find the page. Find the pen. Find the amount again. Who do I write it out to? How much was it again? Then comes the big moment, the signature. The pen hovers and finally touches down for a long, cursive journey through "Mrs. Franklin J. Nelson, Jr."

Just when I can't imagine the procedure extending longer, the customer etches the figures into her check register and rebalances the checkbook right there, on the spot, with a dozen people waiting in line. This means subtracting $24.95 from $24,934.36, a calculation that takes at least another minute or three. By this time, I am pulling out what little hair I have. This excruciating ritual is performed thousands of times daily in stores throughout North America. The cost to the economy can only be imagined.

Now, for my customer's perspective.

Getting to the store was an effort. It took two days to find somebody to drive her here. Some items have been on her list for more than several weeks. The car ride was the first in some time, a sheer delight, a pity it went by so fast. Then, a bracing blast of fresh air on the walk into the store. The utterly exhausting process of locating items and checking and rechecking her list. And, of course, standing in line.

After all this, she is darn well going take her time handing over the check!

Great Aunt Olive

My 102-year-old great aunt Olive maintained a cache of sayings designed to soften almost any situation. As reassuring as Ma Ingalls' "all's well that ends well" in *Little House on the Prairie*, Aunt Olive's adages go back to her youth on the farm. Each has a history.

When Aunt Olive was a teen, her older brother, my grandfather Melvin, converted from his family's Lutheran faith to Baptist. To the mortification of the local Lutherans, he was re-baptized as an adult in the muddy Wild Rice River. The news was duly reported in the local paper.

Their Mama Lena was lenient, a model of tolerance. If Melvin wanted to attend the little Baptist church nearby, more power to him. However, the town gossip mill whirred into motion over Melvin's very public defection. Eventually, old Mrs. Olson called and, in typical Scandinavian manner, didn't immediately bring up the real reason she phoned.

Instead, Mrs. Olson said in a slow, somber tone, "I've been reading the *Times*?"

Mama knew right away what Mrs. Olson had seen in the paper—Melvin's heresy.

Ever after, when somebody they knew ended up in the paper, Mama and Olive would say, slowly, like Mrs. Olson, "I've been reading the *Times*?" and dissolve into giggles.

When I write about Aunt Olive in my column in the local paper, I inevitably get a call from her the day the paper comes out.

"I've been reading the *Times*?" she says, gravely.

The ancient phone call from Mrs. Olson to Mama Lena lives on in Aunt Olive's bank of situational sayings.

When Aunt Olive was in her early twenties, she and her friend Marlys attended a day-long youth rally with other young people from their area. Somehow Gjelmer, a big, friendly but none-too-bright farm boy, had impressed the visiting preacher as being a young man on fire for the Lord. The evangelist anointed Gjelmer with the honor of giving the opening prayer for the last session of the event. But when the moment arrived, poor Gjelmer fell apart. After stuttering around, he burst out with, "Lord help us all until this here gets over with."

Olive and Marlys shook with laughter. And the phrase lived on.

Whenever Aunt Olive gets into a pickle, she leans over and whispers, "Lord help us all until this here gets over with."

Aunt Olive's younger brother Johnny had a heart of gold for all living things—and some not living. When he was five, Johnny adopted a stick that became his pony. He named it Odie. After Mama Lena broke Odie over her knee and threw him in the cookstove for kindling, Johnny wailed bloody murder. Mama apologized, but in vain. Johnny would not be consoled.

Finally, Mama said, "Let's go out in the woods and find another Odie!"

Wiping away the tears, Johnny shook his head.

"There will never be another Odie," he said forlornly.

Since then, Aunt Olive's catch phrase when something gets lost or ruined that she might have actually valued is, "There will never be another Odie!"

Her mock use of the phrase reveals Aunt Olive's philosophy toward all possessions: Things are nice, but losing them isn't a tragedy—unless you are five and lose a stick named Odie.

Recently, Aunt Olive made the local paper. It seems the nursing home took some residents, including Aunt Olive, to Bunny's place at the lake. Paralyzed from the waist down in an accident years ago, Bunny owns a home, dock and pontoon, all handicap accessible. He loves to give the wheelchair-bound nursing home residents rides on his pontoon. During the previous five years, he and Aunt Olive had struck up a little romance, despite a fifty-year age difference.

On the last trip, depending upon whose account you believe, Aunt Olive insisted on kissing Bunny or Bunny insisted Olive kiss him, but no matter, a kiss occurred and was duly reported in the local paper with the editorial comment, "Easy there, old girl!"

When I called Aunt Olive after the scandal had broken, I lowered my voice and said somberly, "I've been reading the *Times*?"

Aunt Olive knew exactly what I referred to.

Grandma Olga

My grandmother Olga lost her memory in her last years. Although she didn't know anybody's name, that didn't lessen the enjoyment of visiting her in the nursing home. Sometimes, she mistook me for her father.

"If you're my father, you know how to speak Swede!" she said with irritation when I couldn't understand her Swedish quotes.

Other times she thought I was her uncle from up north. I did my best to play whatever role she assigned me.

Often, Grandma wasn't interested in pictures of family or in my latest news. In fact, she was just plain uninterested in new stimulation. So I asked her to repeat her Swedish prayer. Immediately, she perked up, closed her eyes in concentration, and recited the entire, beautiful litany. Ever the teacher, she tried to teach it to me. When I mangled the Swedish pronunciations, she corrected me.

"Good enough." She laughed, dismissing my lesser intellect. "I guess it'll have to do."

She never required long visits. She preferred her own company. A couple of repetitions of the prayer were all she needed. The Swedish benediction was a surefire way to reach her. I left with a stronger connection to Grandma.

The prayer formula worked—until I came in for a visit and was intercepted at the door by Grandma's roommate, Amanda, who grabbed me by the arms and said, "I have to talk to you." She backed me into the hallway.

"Whatever you do, please, please do not get your grandmother started on that prayer. Once she gets started, she doesn't stop until four in the morning!"

I honored Amanda's request, but wished Grandma had a private room so she could recite prayers as she wished, all night long if she wanted.

Helen

While playing the piano at a distant nursing home, I was startled to look into the audience and spy an old customer I had not seen in years. Helen had been a missionary in China for four decades and she let everybody know it. Her pious long-suffering continued into retirement, even when it came to growing plants. Her geraniums often died, and Helen thumped her way to the nursery office with her cane. I dreaded her appearances.

She wore bottle-bottom glasses that made her eyes look like those of a large goldfish. I wanted so badly to say, "Helen, I know why your geraniums died. You looked at them!"

But now, her face was considerably softer, possibly because of the old hymns I played.

She knew the words. To test her, I played four verses and heard her warble feebly, wearing a little, beatific smile.

After I finished my program, staff ushered residents to the dining hall for coffee and donuts. Before she rolled off in her wheelchair, I held Helen's hand. "Thanks so much for singing along on the hymns."

Helen looked up through her bottle-bottom glasses with the largest, gentlest goldfish eyes I had ever seen—and didn't say a word. She couldn't. Helen had been forced into the nursing home by a stroke that rendered her speechless.

"But she *sang!*" I said to the aide.

"Yes, she loves to sing," the aide answered as she rolled Helen away.

Crankiness

Grandpa Melvin

In our neighborhood, my grandpa was a big shot and never doubted it. From the time his brother was fourteen and Grandpa was twelve, they managed the family farm. After putting himself through one winter quarter of high school, during which he took a horticulture class, Grandpa started a nursery business from scratch in 1936, at the depth of the Great Depression, and built it to dozens of employees by 1941. His goal was to beautify the barren Red River Valley of the North and sell millions of trees to that end.

After retiring at sixty-two, Grandpa still arrived to work and pursue his own projects. During the spring rush, he helped customers. Many insisted on seeing "the boss," whom they assumed was Grandpa. He didn't mind one bit. However, a new generation of customers saw Dad and Mom as boss, and a few times Grandpa was rudely put in his place.

On a cold April day six years into his retirement, he spotted a customer looking over some trees. He walked out to help the man, who had no idea Grandpa was the founder of the nursery. When Grandpa offered him assistance, the man curtly replied, "No, I would prefer to deal with the boss."

Head hanging, Grandpa turned and shuffled back to the office where he sank into the rocking chair he kept near his desk. Tears streamed down his face. It was a sorry scene, and I didn't know what to make of it. I looked at him with sympathy, but remembered his face smeared with tears whenever he went out in cold weather. Perhaps he wasn't actually crying? I didn't dare ask.

In the end, Grandpa laughed off the customer's insulting refusal to deal with somebody of his low stature, but the rejection clearly hurt. His status was reduced. He knew it was just the beginning. As the years wore on and similar incidents piled up, the slights pushed him from resignation to downright crankiness.

Rosemary

Rosemary was a good customer, but she was a bear to deal with. When she pulled up in her car and got out to help her disabled husband into his cart, we all instinctively recoiled with dread. But she bought plants, and lots of them, so we humored her as best we could.

One busy day at the nursery, Rosemary drove up. No husband this time. An older woman accompanied her. I was filled with dread and Rosemary didn't disappoint. She took no time for pleasantries. "How come your trees are so damn expensive?" she barked.

I was in no mood to take her guff, so for once I shot back, "Because the world is full of gullible people like you who pay!"

"Hmmph!" she snorted and went off to get a donut. When she returned, the corner of her mouth betrayed a hint of a smile. Rosemary knew she could do business with me. Sensing she fancied a little give and take, I continued to answer her questions in the same brusque, cranky manner she asked them. She clearly enjoyed our bantering.

After I stood up to Rosemary, we became friends. I found out she had gone through a lot in life, including caring for her disabled husband for fifteen years before he died. Rosemary had a heart of gold. But she had a sense of dignity as well. Condescension and overbearing solicitude offended her sensibilities.

As I got to know Rosemary, I found out she was a tree expert. She loved trees of every sort. She studied trees. She grew trees, even on their tiny lot in town where she was forced to move after selling the farm to pay her husband's medical expenses. Rosemary knew so much about trees that she was tapped to manage a huge tree planting project for a multi-community school built on the open prairie midway between the towns it served.

Two years after grumbling about our expensive trees, Rosemary sat at her kitchen table negotiating the enormous project she oversaw. She leaned over to me and whispered loudly, "Charge them full price. They've got all the money in the world."

Amanda

"I love the cranky ones," said my high school classmate Michelle Gunufson, who has worked at the local nursing home for thirty-two years. "They are the ones who become your best friends."

She cited the case of Amanda, who had been my grandmother's roommate.

Amanda was notoriously cranky. She told anybody who would listen that she was kicked in the temple by a horse when she was a child; the injury severed the nerve that allowed her to smile. So cranky was Amanda, nobody suspected she would use that muscle much anyway.

But Amanda had one of the most amazing minds Michelle and I ever encountered. She remembered every date and every event in her life.

"What happened today?" I asked Amanda. She knew what I meant and rattled off the list: In 1947, the pastor at Little Norway Church resigned. In 1956, Mervin Johnson lost his leg in a car accident. In 1936, Franklin Roosevelt gave a fireside chat. It was the birthday of Herman Nelson. Josie and Roger Clark got married in a rainstorm this day in 1968.

Amanda knew it all. And the key to her heart was to create the opportunity for her to recite some of it. She was never brusque with me again.

Michelle had a similar experience. Their friendship grew to the point that Amanda insisted other nurses call Michelle, or "Mrs. Gunufson" as Amanda called her, to make sure things were right with her medications and care.

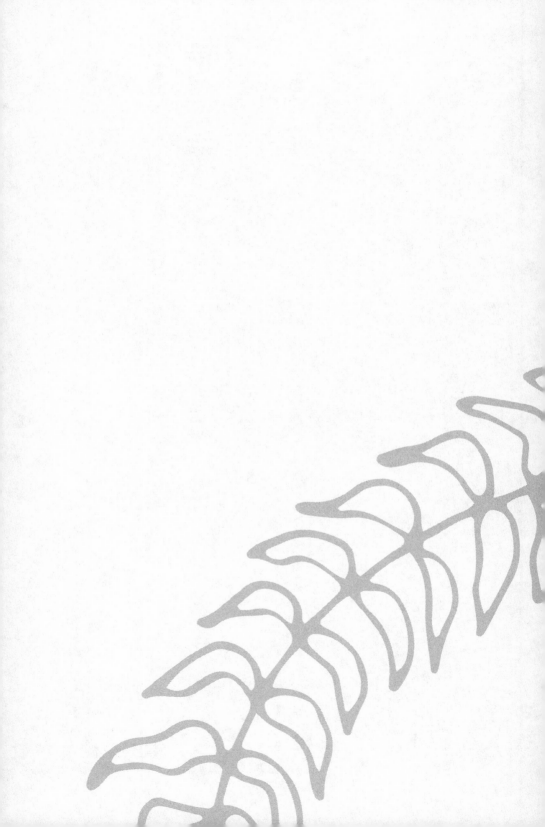

Alliances

Annie and Hector Hanson

Intoxicated by wafts of freshly cut grass, I ambled down Main Street one June evening. I hadn't gone four blocks when I heard a screech from the Hanson's porch.

"Hey, you!" yelled Annie Hanson. "Get up here!"

Annie was laughing. But she meant it. She was on the porch with her husband, Hector, sipping lemonade—the very sort of white-picket-fence activity you don't imagine happens any more.

Annie and Hector were about town, but I had never sat down with them. Hector always had a fishing cap attached to his head. He squinted as if looking into the distance and wore a permanent sneer, which I soon learned was a misleading mistake of creation. Hector was a gentleman, and I was shocked to learn he was ninety-years-old.

I pulled up a chair, Annie fetched more lemonade, and Hector and I had our first visit. The topic was politics. To my surprise,

I learned Hector had served in the Minnesota legislature during World War II. After two terms, he retired and became the postmaster of the House of Representatives in the State Capitol Building for many years, remaining at the center of state politics without having to go through the trouble of seeking election. Despite his long absence from the House, Hector knew some of the senior staff I met when I worked at the Capitol decades later.

Hector was a good old Minnesota liberal, a believer in what government can do, not what it shouldn't do, so we had plenty to talk about. Old Hector sat there squinting, spouting wisdom and history. The late evening sun set before I left. Annie urged me to visit again.

As if reminded by my visit to fill her flowerpots, the very next day Annie arrived at the nursery for geraniums. She screeched, as usual, but her message was that Hector really enjoyed our visit and I should come back soon.

And, Annie said, Hector was dying of bone cancer.

A couple of weeks passed. I walked down the street again. Hector and Annie sat on their porch. We had another glass of lemonade. Hector was a little weaker.

Two weeks later, it was raining and we couldn't work, so I called Annie. Come on over, she screeched. Hector would love to see you. This time he had two books about the United States Senate in the 1950s he wanted to loan me. My recently-finished master's thesis centered on U. S. Senator William Langer of North Dakota, who served from 1941-1959, so Hector had chosen the books according to my interest.

He was notably weaker at each visit.

One day Annie called and asked if I couldn't come cheer him up a bit. I did. And five days later, Annie called to say he had died.

All told, Hector and I visited five times over the space of three months. After the first visit, I knew he wasn't long for this world, but the only mention he made to me of his illness during our visits was that he was tired and it was no fun. Annie told me of his great pain, typical of bone cancer. I still have his books on the U. S. Senate. I treasure them both.

My short friendship with Hector remains a valued memory. Although you think you know everybody in the small town, you don't know everybody's story. Some older folks are pretty tight-lipped. Many don't think anybody cares about the history stored in their heads. But most have fascinating stories. Hector was one of the first older people in town to take me seriously enough to con-duct a political discussion, to loan me a book, to tell me his stories.

That summer with him reminded me of other summer relation-ships, namely those formed at Bible Camp.

Summer camp was a place to meet new people. One week spent in a nest of shabby cabins with kids my age was a break from the isolation on the farm. Magical friendships and golden memories formed. Part of the enchantment of summer camp was the scenery and the freedom, but something else contributed to the frenzy: We knew the friendships ended in a week. Sure, we could write each other letters, but for all practical purposes, once we left camp Saturday afternoon, it would be at least one year until we saw each other again, if ever.

Ah, the summer camp romances and relationships. For one week, anybody could hide his worst self, his most boring self, the self somebody might not like. For one week, we overlooked signs of trouble, of possessiveness, of clinginess, of abusive behavior and other slow cancers that corrode friendships over the long haul.

As the sun set on our fourth visit, I realized my relationship with Hector was a summer camp friendship. He would be dead by winter. Although never mentioned, his demise changed the way we talked.

Short, limited friendships. They are the stuff of great memories. The person on the plane. The study date with a classmate in American

Literature 350 that turned into an all-night bull session. The fellow hitchhiker in the New Zealand wilderness. And, a very old person watching the sun set on his last days.

Mervin

A local hardware man, long retired, Mervin died at ninety-four after several years in a nursing home. His wife died forty years earlier of cancer. Mervin was prematurely stooped during my youth, and I viewed him as very old from the very beginning. He was dignified, careful, and dutiful to his community.

Mervin and I became buddies. I shared a first name with his grandson, who was my age. Mervin reminded me of that every time we visited. I came to idealize my alter ego Eric and was thrilled to meet him at Mervin's funeral, decades later.

Funerals are a weekly event in my small town, and I avoid most of them or I'd get nothing else done. But I decided to go to Mervin's due to our friendship thirty years earlier.

Slipping into the back pew just as the service started, I was surprised to see Marjorie, a beautiful local waitress, in the same row. We both looked out of place and were relieved the other showed up, probably the only non-family members under seventy in the entire church.

As the family exited after the service, I asked her how she knew Mervin. A young widow and mother, she told me she had lost her husband in a farm accident three years before. Her recovery from her husband's death was slow. The marriage had been contentious and she was blamed by many and treated rudely.

As a part of her recovery, Marjorie volunteered at a nursing home thirty miles away where the gossip couldn't follow. Mervin was a resident in the same facility.

Like Marjorie, he lost his spouse at an early age and his marriage saw rough waters. As you can imagine, it is difficult to talk about a deceased spouse with whom you had difficulty. Most prefer to idealize the dead person, neatly wrapping the topic, plopping a bow of sentiment on top, and calling it good.

Mervin and Marjorie found common ground. They talked for hours. Marjorie's volunteer time was spent mostly with him, playing games, putting together puzzles, laughing, and talking.

Adolf

Adolf loved baseball. Although he was in his nineties and almost completely deaf and blind, he attended every game our Legion baseball team played. Not only did he show up for home games, he appeared for away games. Somebody must have leaked the information to his wife. We let him on the bus without question. He never said a word. He sat in the front seat and leaned on the knob of his cane. With a shrug, we made him our mascot.

Adolf sat with us in the dugout, likely unaware of what was going on. We put him where he would be sheltered from a foul ball because he sure wouldn't see one coming.

One of our last games was in the town of Bagley. The crowd was small but rowdy. The game got a little rough. The crowd jeered our team and the tougher guys on our bench jeered back. Back in that time, fistfights in the stands weren't unheard of, and things were headed in that direction.

Ping! went an aluminum bat. It was a foul pop, over the screen and into the crowd behind home plate. Because there were only three balls at each Legion game, the ball had to be retrieved before play could continue. Getting the ball back meant more interaction between players and fans. Everybody's attention was on the stands while somebody chased the ball.

Meanwhile, Adolf needed to take a leak. During the rare moment when nobody was watching, Adolf wandered out to a spot five feet behind home plate. When a fan threw the ball over the screen back to the catcher, everybody's eyes followed the ball down to home plate where old Adolf had unzipped his pants and started to pee.

There was only one thing to do; a few players encircled him, facing outward, and let him finish what he'd started. The combative mood was broken. The game continued without further incident.

Grandma Olga

Although my Grandma Olga didn't come across as a warm person at first blush, she cared for people in her own stern, firm way. A strict temperance advocate, Grandma had no tolerance for drinking, swearing, and smoking. She also couldn't abide small talk. Get to the point!

When we all lived on the farm, my Uncle Albert and Aunt Eleanor would stop by, always unannounced, in their big camper. Aunt Eleanor was a specimen. Cussing, grousing, and constantly smoking from the minute she arrived, she made sure everybody knew she didn't want to be on our farm. I wonder if *she* knew how welcome she was to leave!

Although no blood relation, Aunt Eleanor and Grandma Olga bonded. What a relief for us when the camper pulled up and, after a few choice words, Aunt Eleanor padded to Grandma's kitchen in her flip-flops, trailing smoke from her Virginia Slims. I ran through Grandma's kitchen to find the two taciturn women looking happier than you'd ever seen them. They were unlikely birds of a feather.

On staff when Grandma moved to the nursing home, Ophelia was a rough woman from an old-fashioned farm. She not only worked a full-time job, she milked the cows and fed the farm animals when she got home. Then she made supper for her husband. Lord knows what he ever did; Ophelia did all the work and made all the money. She was missing teeth and talked in poor English. Her loud, somewhat uncouth manner offended many.

But Ophelia didn't offend Grandma Olga. They bonded long before Grandma's memory left her, back when Ophelia frequented the nursery. She often snuffed out her cigarette and walked up to the house to sit at the kitchen table with Grandma for a no-nonsense conversation. So it was no surprise that even when Grandma was in her nineties and had no memory of anything or anybody, the staff member most able to bring a smile was crusty, rough Ophelia.

Great Aunt Olive

Routine builds trust. Ask the substitute UPS man if he can do anything right when he fills in for Phil, the regular driver who knows to put the package inside the back screen door. Ask the replacement for Marsha, the business-like aide who knows just how tight to tie shoes.

Sometimes competence is more important than trust.

"I know she's stealing me blind," Aunt Olive said of a housekeeper, "but she's the only one who does a decent job of scrubbing the bathroom."

Aunt Olive's gut reaction was right: There was something vaguely untrustworthy about the cleaning lady (who we know was not stealing her blind, because Aunt Olive had nothing of value to steal). However, so rare was it to find somebody who could actually scrub a bathroom properly, Aunt Olive thought her worth the risk of a pair of cheap earrings disappearing.

Toxicity

Bertram

When I attended college near his home, a retired English teacher befriended me. A delightful curmudgeon, Bertram smoked long cigarettes and offered wry observations on world affairs.

He took me out for dinner. I was barely eighteen, in an era when identification was not needed to drink booze, and Bertram enjoyed buying me martinis. After two, my 130-lb. body entered a state of pleasant numbness, and I earnestly talked about the poems assigned in my American literature class. We both enjoyed the conversation.

Before leaving the restaurant on one visit, we both went in the men's room. Old Bertram made his move. Even in my naivety, his intentions became obvious. He got me tipsy in order to take advantage of me. I pushed him away. I felt disgusted and betrayed. I never spoke to him again, nor did he attempt contact. Eventually, he entered a nursing home about fifty miles from my home. Never married, he had few relatives or friends other than some old ladies at church. When I went to visit his nursing home to play piano, he never came out to listen. Nor did I go see him.

Eventually, I saw his obituary. It filled me with relief, and I realized that not all friendships with elderly people are easy or even worth continuing.

Myra

Myra has lived alone for decades, her ramshackle house surrounded by brush and weeds. Children around town call her a witch. Now in her upper eighties, she can barely get out of bed to cook herself a meal. She could easily be in assisted living, but refuses. She could have housecleaning and home health subsidized by the county, but she spurns the offers.

My friendship with Myra lasted ten years. It started at the nursery when she arrived in a cape with a flowing feather boa. A diva to end all divas, she made her demands known as if she were Cleopatra in the Shakespearean play. Always eager to meet somebody interesting, I became Myra's friend. Eventually, I was invited to her home, straight from a Victorian movie set. Jammed with books, trinkets, antiques (which to Myra were still functional), LPs, blankets, curtains, cushions and lace, the four-story house was clean but utterly overrun with stuff. Elsewhere were mementoes from her time spent in the Mideast. In the attic, Arabian cushions surrounded a multi-hosed Hookah pipe that looked like Medusa.

Myra loved to cook ethnic feasts. The first I attended was a Lebanese affair. It took Myra a month to concoct all the dishes. She researched every recipe and painstakingly wrote out the menu in her Victorian handwriting, including the history of each dish and its ingredients. The twenty-five-page document was bound with pink ribbon and placed on the chair of each guest. New diners were often moved to tears by Myra's herculean effort to make the meal. There were toasts all around as we moved into the living room for more drinks before dessert, which alone consisted, in one instance, of five dishes.

I was invited to at least five of Myra's majestic and mysterious dinners. After we finished with Algeria, Lebanon, and Ethiopia, we moved to Ireland.

The Irish feast would end our friendship.

Myra badly wanted to teach me to cook. I eventually, and reluctantly, agreed. We were to spend an entire day preparing the meal. The date was set months in advance. I was to buy the ingredients, including a bone-in standing rib roast. Never mind that there is no longer such a thing on the market. It was my job to find one.

I could not. I could only find a boneless roast. Myra heaped contempt on my head over the phone.

The day we cooked started badly and got progressively worse. Despite her Bohemian life, which included affairs with jazz musicians on Mediterranean islands and time spent with beatniks in San Francisco, when it came to interpreting a recipe book, Myra was an angry, literal-minded fundamentalist.

The day of cooking was filled with abuse. I took every bit in stride, or so I thought. Evening came, some mutual friends arrived, and the meal was served. One guest was Myra's son. He got drunk and compared the meal, which in my estimation had turned out reasonably well, to bird feces, axle grease, and carrion. Myra gleefully agreed and blamed me for everything.

My reservoir of humor ran dry. I nearly punched the son.

Looking back, I think Myra set me up. A socialist, anarchist and whatever else she could call herself to shock and dismay the sturdy but boring folk of her town, she deeply despised my business career. Bestowed with a brilliant mind for literature, music and art, Myra had the emotional maturity of a twelve-year-old. After the miserable, day-long ordeal of cooking a meal under her merciless tutelage and eating it under a barrage of insults, I decided the children of the town were probably right in their assessment.

Myra was a witch.

We spoke on the phone once more, a week after the Irish feast fiasco. She apologized half-heartedly—for the wrong things. I left for the winter and wrote Myra a long letter. She loved to correspond in her old-school handwriting and formal, Shakespearean prose and always responded within days.

This time, I heard nothing.

The feeling was mutual. Our friendship was over.

We have no enmity. I saw her once in the past ten years when her son asked me to help him clean her yard. I met her in the den, where we had spent so many long evenings laughing, smoking cigarettes, reading aloud—and felt a few pangs of nostalgia. Then I realized: Our friendship had run its course.

The Irish feast was Myra's way of kicking me out of her life. By accepting her invitation to leave, I made a painful decision. I was lonely for Myra for about a year. Then, stories filtered down from mutual friends who had also been dumped, her pattern for decades. I was not the first, nor was I to be the last. I felt fortunate that I had taken the hint. Others stuck around for more pain.

Grandpa Melvin

Grandpa taught me almost everything I know about connecting with elderly people, often by presenting problems I had to solve at an unnaturally early age.

I drew the line with Grandpa when he tried to take over my daily life. I controlled my anger when he faked heart attacks to get me to visit the nursing home—immediately. I asserted myself to maintain my own existence when he wanted me to take off from my graduate studies to co-author his book. I controlled my fury when he insisted Saturday nights were the ideal time to pick choke-cherries, at an hour curiously close to the time I wanted to leave for a drive-in movie with my high school buddies.

All through my childhood, adolescence and young adulthood, I feared I inadequately met Grandpa's needs. He ensured I would never feel good enough. If I visited twice a week, he expected three. If I visited four times a week, he wanted five. Grandpa loomed over my life for the last twenty years of his.

The night Grandpa died, as I drove away from the nursing home to go home and start calling friends and relatives with the news, I felt as if a thunderstorm had passed. I was sad, but oh-so-relieved. The long reign of terror was over. I was now free to be my own person.

Yet two nights later, when I turned on the radio and heard old Herb Carneal announcing a Twins game, I recalled the good times Grandpa and I had had talking baseball. I cried. We'd been friends, too.

Having served Grandpa for twenty years (a short length of time compared to Grandma's sixty years of service) and subsumed my being to his ego, I felt so liberated by his absence that I avoided older people for the next three years. I wanted nothing to do with the manipulation, the guilt, the drama, the self-pity, the black hole of demands. Without thinking, I unfairly blamed all of the elderly in my life, including my grandmother, for my subservient relation-ship with Grandpa.

Other family members and nursing home staff took good care of Grandma. She got along without me. Contrary to my self-aggrandizing belief that only I could adequately tend her, others capably stepped in. Only as she approached death did I start visiting her regularly. Those few visits delighted me.

Since Grandma's death, I have become friends with many, many very old people, most notably Aunt Olive, Grandpa's younger sister. Aunt Olive displays some of Grandpa's traits, but only one-tenth the degree. However, instead of running the other way when Olive wants something done, I relish the opportunity to do what I didn't do with Grandpa—either help without inner complaint, or draw the line.

During his last decade, my grandfather sent out a monthly inspirational newsletter to a mailing list of one hundred people he had met over the years at Bible Camps, retreats, and the like. Although he struck some addresses and added others each month, the number stayed equal to one roll of stamps.

He typed single-spaced, border-to-border, and sometimes up the side. On the back he copied two hymns of the month.

Many, many times, Grandpa attempted to solicit help from others. I agreed at times to find the right hymns or to copy the letters. One time, and only one time, I hand-addressed all one hundred envelopes. I sometimes took the bundle to the post office.

However, as Grandpa declined, he got bossier about the newsletter. Once, he decided I should write the epistle so it could continue after his death!

Well, I shared neither Grandpa's theology nor his need to maintain a monthly correspondence to *his* acquaintances. It just wasn't my bag.

I realized what was going on. Grandpa was in a down mood; he scrounged for indications his work on this earth had been worthwhile. The newsletter was the least of his contributions to the world, but it was, in his last year, a symbol of his importance. Even knowing that, I struggled to keep my cool.

Grandpa's demand to take over starting *now* touched so many of my hot buttons. As I entered adulthood, I was more sensitive to being treated as an appendage. I finally started to respect my own time and realize I had the right to reserve the bulk of it for myself.

So, I stalled.

I said let's talk about it next week. After that week, I said nobody could replace him, and his old friends really wanted to hear from him, anyway. By then, Grandpa had recovered from his desperate mood and composed the next newsletter himself. When he died several months later, we found three newsletters he had written in advance. My mother dutifully duplicated them and we mailed them to his list. And that was the end of it.

We also discovered the last installment of his column "Garden Tips" for the local paper. I took it to the publisher with the news Grandpa had passed away.

A few weeks later, the publisher phoned. "Could you take over your grandpa's column?"

I was reluctant. I was not the gardener Grandpa was. But I agreed to try.

I wrote about gardening for three weeks. Then I veered off into other topics. The publisher gave me full leeway by naming the column "Down on the Farm" without discussing it with me. I took advantage and wrote about whatever I wanted. Within a few years, the column appeared in twenty-two papers and I had published a book of collected columns, which sold 5,000 copies.

It took a while to admit I merely widened the trail blazed by Grandpa.

Forgiveness

Henry Helm

Henry Helm lived across the road from the nursery in a rusty, tin-sided house, sunk in a swamp with potential to be a malarial hollow if it were in the tropics. A wiry German, he wore big boots, drab work shirts, and pulled his leather belt tight around his twenty-four-inch waist. He took long steps and always had a Salem dangling from his lip.

And, as I learned the hard way, Henry had no time for children. When Dad took over the nursery, he inherited Grandpa's crew of grizzled older men. Henry was one of them. On a summer day when I was seven, Dad rounded up a crew to dig spruce trees down at the corner plot. As they gathered burlap, spades and nails, I begged to go along. Dad, frazzled by the frenzy, didn't hear me, but Henry did. He stuck his bony, calloused finger in my chest and said, "You stay here or I'll bury you up to your neck and leave you."

He wasn't kidding.

Just then, Dad turned to me and said, "You'd better stay home, Eric."

I nearly peed my pants. I ran to the trailer house and threw myself on the couch. Only seven years old and I had barely escaped death. Henry would have buried me and Dad didn't have the power to stop him! I feared Henry for the next two years, an eternity to a child.

Four years later, I wanted desperately to watch the 1975 World Series, but neither my parents nor grandparents had a television. Grandpa knew that Henry, despite otherwise living in abject poverty, did own a large color set, one of the first in the neighborhood. Against my wishes, Grandpa called Henry to see if we could come over to watch the first game. My stomach sank. To make things worse, Grandpa got busy working and said, "You go yourself. Henry's expecting you."

As I walked into the swampy hollow, I felt as if I was headed for the guillotine. By this time, Mom and Dad had built a new house and sold our trailer to Henry. The old, rust-covered tin house was abandoned, entangled with vines. In only two years, our trailer had succumbed to Henry's widower ways. Two of the mirrors in the living room were shattered. Caked pots and pans covered the kitchen counter. The dining room table was covered in crumbs, bills, and newspapers.

Henry cleared a spot for me on the couch.

Oh, how I hoped he would leave and let me watch the game alone and not shoot me with one of his shotguns. But he stayed. And made me lemonade. It was the first baseball game I had ever watched in color. Pot-bellied Cuban pitcher Luis Tiant of the Red Sox tantalized the Cincinnati Reds with slow curves before zapping them with his fastball. I had never seen anything like it. And by the seventh inning of the Red Sox victory, I felt pretty comfortable sitting in the same room—alone with Henry. I began to suspect I would live to tell about it.

Henry and I made our peace that day and were on speaking terms for the last four years of his life. One year later, I came into our house to a big bag of beautiful red apples. We had plenty of apple trees on our nursery, but none of them bore apples that looked store-bought. Where did we get these? I asked. "Henry brought them over from his tree," Mom said.

I couldn't imagine such an act of neighborliness and charity from somebody as gruff as Henry. He not only made me lemonade and let me watch the World Series, but now he gave us apples. Big, red, juicy Beacon apples, the best there were.

One winter day in 1979, after everybody else had been dropped off, school bus-driver Art gestured for me to come up front.

"So, you lost a neighbor today," he said, his gaze fixed on Henry's ramshackle farm.

Henry had died. He didn't decline, he just died, probably due to general neglect of his health and a long life lived hard.

Thanks to the Red Sox game, which was the only time I ever sat down with Henry, I was more sorry than relieved. Joseph Stalin once said the best friendships are based on a solved misunderstanding. He might well have added, if you don't bury the friend alive first!

By the following August, Henry's swampy homestead was overgrown in weeds. Summer's heat and rain reduced the driveway to two mud ruts barely visible beneath the rustling reeds of canary grass. His trailer had been pulled away. The rusty tin house and the sagging barn remained. I walked down the drive to his old apple tree, hoping to sneak a couple Beacons on the sly.

After forging through the face-high grass, I arrived at the apple tree and stopped cold. It was dead. Like Henry, it hadn't survived the winter. The tree was now a good memory, like the fall afternoon spent watching the World Series on Henry's couch.

Norris

As I walked into the town junk store to rummage for a chair, I noticed a familiar, rusted-orange pickup parked outside. For years, I had watched the Datsun drive past our nursery almost daily, but I had never met its occupant, neighbor Norris Jacobson.

Inside the store was a group of old men visiting. I picked out the only man I didn't recognize and extended my hand.

"Norris? Eric Bergeson."

"Well, if it isn't a Bergeson," he replied.

"Nice to meet you," I said, nervous.

I brought up the only topic of conversation that seemed possible between us: Norris' war experience.

"I hear you drove Jeep for General Patton."

"Not Patton, exactly, but a few others," Norris replied. "It wasn't glamorous."

From his wallet, Norris dug out a wrinkled black and white photograph. "Take a look."

The picture showed skeletal Holocaust victims, eyes wide in sunshine that seemed too much for them to bear, huddled against the slatboard building, which likely had been their prison.

"I have kept that in my wallet since the war."

Even though he hadn't been part of the force that liberated the camps, he had visited them later and kept the picture because, "I needed reminding why we had to go over there."

As more people entered the dusty shop, pressure mounted on us to join the general conversation.

"Stop by the nursery sometime!" I said, making sure to look Norris in the eye.

"I will," he said, meeting my gaze.

I knew Norris would keep his promise. I also knew it would be the first time he had set foot on the nursery in over forty years of driving past.

Norris had returned from the war to find things changed on the farm. The small family he started with Selma could no longer make ends meet on a 160-acre plot. So he farmed his land on the side while holding down a full-time job at Bergeson Nursery, one-and-a-half miles from home.

Selma worked at the nursery, too. Wages weren't high, but Grandpa fed his crew hearty meals, which added extra value to their jobs.

Like many boys off the farm in that era, Norris was a genius with machines. He could build anything. Most of the nursery's cultivators (there were dozens) and outbuildings (at least a dozen) bore Norris' stamp.

After a time, something happened between Norris and Grandpa. I have never figured out what, except to know Grandpa eventually parted ways with all of his best men. He couldn't stand anybody else having an opinion. He refused to delegate authority. He couldn't abide others making decisions, no matter how qualified they were. That would have been fine if Grandpa had been able to make a decision himself. But because he always changed his mind, the most capable employees tried to make decisions without bringing the matter before Grandpa. Grandpa was on the road a lot. The trick often worked.

But not always.

Norris was amply qualified to make decisions and he knew it. At some point, I suspect Norris made a decision while Grandpa was napping at the house or on the road, and when Grandpa found out, the shit hit the fan.

All I knew for sure was that three years before I was born, Norris took Selma, left the nursery, and never spoke to Grandpa again.

In forty years of living just over a mile apart, I had somehow never encountered Norris on the street, at the fair, at a funeral, or even in a lonely snow bank halfway to town during a blizzard, a common place for feuding prairie neighbors to be forced to melt the ice.

Norris and his daughter arrived at the nursery only a couple of days after I bumped into Norris at the junk store. I made every attempt to welcome him grandly without overdoing it, without bringing up the missing decades. Some of the cultivators Norris built fifty years earlier still nestled in the weeds. We ambled past them. By now, my father and mother had cleaned up most of the old buildings, shanties, and shacks. Norris told stories about what used to be there.

The subject of Grandpa didn't come up. Nothing was said about whatever happened between them. We visited for an hour and said goodbye as if we were old neighbors. Which we were.

I never spoke with Norris again. He died that winter. He was in his mid-eighties. I am glad we met at the junk store when we did.

Reynold

Reynold was a pillar of the community who owned a Main Street business. He was chief of the Fire Department and served for decades on the Polk County Fair Board.

At some point, nobody knows when, he must have made some money. When I was in high school in the 1980s, Reynold purchased a brand new Lincoln Continental every year. Reynold was tall, dignified, and proper, with fresh-combed hair and an ice blue stare. In his car, he looked downright imposing.

Each year, our high school play was a lollapalooza, the big event for non-athletes and athletes, too—the whole town, for that matter. Mr. Rickey, our play director, made us think it was the biggest production outside of Broadway. We believed him.

After years of procuring props for the annual play, Mr. Rickey had an encyclopedic knowledge of every musty attic in the school district. One of the richest troves of antiques was the home of Reynold and Evie, who generously allowed the students to use whatever they needed.

For the production of "Annie Get Your Gun," Mr. Rickey requested three live pigeons. The props committee industriously found an abandoned barn and developed a method to trap the pigeons inside it. With the technology in place, they figured, why stop at three? The committee returned to the school with nineteen birds, properly caged.

Mr. Rickey was not amused. He commanded the props committee to release the excess pigeons immediately.

Meanwhile, old Reynold pulled up to the school with some props in his new car.

With Reynold inside the gym conferring with Mr. Rickey, the props committee decided, after brief deliberation, to deposit the sixteen pigeons into his Lincoln Continental and adjourn for the hills.

Nobody was on hand to see how Reynold reacted when he opened his car door. We do know he said nothing to Mr. Rickey, for if he had, there would have been hell to pay. But the incident never arose.

Years later, Reynold drove Evie out to the nursery to pick up her flowers. I couldn't resist. Without mentioning my possible role in the pigeon affair, I said something to him about possibly hearing something about sometime in the past when possibly there were pigeons in his car.

He chuckled.

"Pretty clever," he said, much to my surprise.

After Reynold passed away, I found out that before he became a man of property and substance, he was known around town for his practical jokes. For example, during the Depression, when young men didn't have jobs or much else to do, Reynold and a buddy got one of those one hundred foot cloth measuring tapes and a box of chalk and walked around town solemnly measuring. After each computation, they put a big X in chalk on a building, on the sidewalk, or on the curb. Not even private homes were spared.

"What's this all about?" asked passers-by.

"Government project," Reynold replied. "WPA."

"What kind of project?"

"Can't say. Top secret."

It led me to wonder if Reynold's first reaction to seeing the sixteen pigeons in his Lincoln was to snort, "Amateurs!"

Dementia

Thelma and Teresa

Thelma was a queenly woman, even in her old age. Thirty years ago, I knew her only as the mother of a high school friend, Teresa.

The only two women in their house, mother and daughter were close. In tender moments, Thelma ran her hands through Teresa's hair, even after she matured into adulthood.

Teresa married my friend Mark and moved to the East Coast. Each summer they returned home to Minnesota to visit.

Eventually Teresa's dad died. Teresa hoped her mother would at least be able to enjoy some leisure in her old age. Unfortunately, without familiar caregiving duties to ground her, Thelma immediately showed symptoms of memory loss and confusion and was diagnosed with Alzheimer's disease. Family disconnected her stove, neighbors watched her closely, and Teresa frequently flew home to see her.

Adept at covering gaps in conversation when memory failed her, Thelma still dressed in her regal manner, white hair coiffed to perfection. Who cared if names escaped her, or if the cereal box landed in the refrigerator.

She continued to deteriorate. Eventually, she lost command of basic words. Sentences became fragmented. She was confused, troubled, fussy at times.

For a while, Thelma lived in independent senior housing, which, fortunately, was attached to the nursing home. A former employee, she found the surroundings familiar. Friendly staff allowed her to wear her old nametag and "come to work" to fold towels each day. She called it "going to church." Nobody corrected her.

Eventually Thelma moved into the nursing home.

In the early stages of her disease, Thelma drew on the same store of reassuring phrases and aphorisms that had gotten her through a difficult life:

"I guess that's just how it goes!"

"You just never know!"

"We'll have to see!"

When Thelma's memory failed her in the middle of a story, she finished with, "and so on and so forth."

When I went to the nursing home to see my great aunt, I enjoyed visiting Thelma, too. After a time, she responded to tone more than content. I opened my arms wide and said, "Well, well, well, look who's here!" as if encountering her was the best surprise of my week. The more I did it, the more it became absolutely true. Thelma laughed and shook her head as if I was, indeed, the most welcome sight in *her* day.

Yet, when Teresa arrived and said, "I am your daughter," Thelma looked blank. Her mother's incomprehension hurt her daughter deeply.

In a response typical of the offspring of Alzheimer's victims, Teresa was angry, angry that her mother—in her mid-seventies—had been deprived of a normal old age. She stopped flying back to visit. But when she developed a serious health problem of her own and felt bereft without her mother to confide in, she became more determined to connect.

When Teresa and Mark returned to Minnesota for the summer, her anger lessened as she slowly accepted her mother as she was and was not hurt by what she wasn't. After all, we're all in slow decline, she told me.

Her first visit to the nursing home went fine. "I didn't call her Mom. I didn't want to confuse her."

At the end of their summer stay, I happened to be at the nursing home the afternoon Teresa and Mark came to say their goodbyes.

We rolled Thelma in her wheelchair to the gazebo in the courtyard. She was distracted. Trucks roared by on the county highway, causing her to look their way. A lady walking a dog drew her attention. As we settled down, Teresa tried to engage her mother with iPad pictures of family gatherings.

"This is Angie." She pointed, hoping Thelma would show a flash of recognition. Instead, she seemed confused.

By now we had taken our seats. The woman with the dog had moved out of sight. The passing trucks took a break. Teresa brought out a gift wrapped in crispy tissue paper, festooned with a delicate bow.

In the manner of older women who kept house through hard times, Thelma gently undid the bow and set it aside. She carefully lifted the Scotch tape, one piece at a time, preserving the fragile wrapping paper.

Totally absorbed, she no longer looked frustrated. She was in a realm of competence. Of familiarity. She unfolded a beautiful blue blouse.

"Oh!" she said, in her you-shouldn't-have voice.

She looked at Teresa and confabulated some mumbo-jumbo that Teresa decided to translate as, "Only you would know my favorite color."

Then came the big moment.

With the rest of us looking on, Thelma reached up and stroked her daughter's hair, just as she had throughout the years.

"You are my..." Thelma stopped, searching the far corners of her language ability.

"Bobo!" she ended triumphantly.

Although the word was new, we all understood the meaning.

And I knew the real gift wasn't the blouse. It was the moment. Beautiful and bittersweet.

Agnes and Margaret

An old Ford station wagon pulled up and parked across the yard at the nursery. An elderly woman with a cane struggled out with the help of her younger relatives and started across the yard toward the office. She looked like a real character, so I walked out to greet the entire crew. The younger ones shyly said hello, but the elderly mother had no such restraint. When I asked her how she was, she loudly announced, "I would be great, but my goddamn knee is giving me hell!"

Not only was her goddamn knee giving her hell, the woman was no longer able to milk her herd of 170 cows.

I knew she was in an altered reality.

The family, to my surprise and delight, simply grinned as the woman tore into her stories, most of them preposterous and all of them delightful. Due to her goddamn knee, the woman took a seat in the checkout area, and not just any seat. She sat right next to the donut pan and helped herself.

Between ringing customers at the till, I continued to ask the woman about her dairy herd, the 170 cows she used to milk herself until her goddamn knee started acting up. Why she milked them that long she didn't know, for she had $650,000 in the bank and didn't need the money. Something about the car she arrived in with her kin indicated to me the $650,000 figure was a little high. But we had a great conversation while she downed donuts.

Then, a second car arrived. Agnes and Margaret, long-time customers from a town forty miles away, were friends, I decided, due to their shared crabbiness. Grumble and moan, mumble and groan was all they ever did. I finally took to asking each time they arrived, "So, what's your problem today?" because there *always* was a problem. (I know now their crankiness is an act, because they always stay around to talk, and it is fun to see if I can get their frowns to crack. But at the time, I wasn't glad to see them).

Agnes was wound as tight as a spring on a garage door. Her white hair always in a perfect beehive, not a strand straying from the cotton ball, a perky contrast to her wrinkled scowl.

"I have to get a donut," she replied to my greeting.

With that, she headed toward the talkative woman sitting guard over the donut pan.

"How are you?" Agnes said gruffly. She lifted the cover of the donut pan.

"Oh, I'd be fine if my goddamn knee wasn't giving me such hell!" said the woman with dementia.

Agnes grumbled, grabbed a donut and replaced the cover with a clang.

At this point, the woman sensed, accurately, that Agnes didn't like her, or anybody else for that matter, and she also sensed something else: Agnes's perfect hair was central to her uptight personality. She went for the jugular.

"So sorry to see your hair is out of place!" she said as loud as she said everything else.

Whoa! Agnes whipped her head around and gave the dairy herder a stare that would shatter glass.

I started to laugh, but could see that wasn't going over well with Agnes and Margaret, so I extricated myself stage right to the gift shop.

As the woman continued to spout about her cows and bundle of money, Agnes realized that she was not in touch with reality. It eased the pain of the woman's hurtful accusation. But nothing will erase my memory of Agnes's face when the woman with Alzheimer's insulted her hair.

Evelyn

When I visited the nursing home after my grandparents entered, I dilly-dallied on the way down the hall to their room at the very end. I became friends with those who sat along the walls in their wheelchairs. My favorite was Evelyn, who had dementia.

At the time, it was still permissible to use restraints, and Evelyn was held into her wheelchair by a tray, which she couldn't unfasten. Oh, how she hated that tray. She grasped it with her pudgy hands. She glowered when it wouldn't budge.

I made it my game to get Evelyn to smile.

I pulled a chair next to hers, sat down, and scowled back. Really scowled. Evelyn realized she was being teased and eventually her expression broke.

One time, Evelyn reached over and pinched my pants right above the knee.

"Nice trousers you've got there." She shook the fabric in her grip.

"Well, thank you, Evelyn," I said.

"No!" she interrupted, panicked. "Keep 'em on!"

We both dissolved into laughter. The ice was broken. Evelyn howled until she was out of breath.

And then she sighed.

"That was some happiness," she said, as if to sum up the whole episode.

Genius! In a drab world where Evelyn was under restraint, both of us just enjoyed some happiness.

Before developing Alzheimer's disease, Evelyn was a prim, proper, and reserved woman who tended to slink into the background of the clattering kitchen when the church women served funerals. She had a nice smile, but she could barely bring herself to say hello. With dementia, Evelyn was hell on wheels, commenting acidly on the appearance of the nurses who passed by, making off-color cracks to men, generally stirring up mischief.

It took me some time to realize Evelyn's family didn't think her new personality was funny. To them, it was tragic. Her sweet, calm presence, the presence that had made them who they were, was gone, replaced by somebody unfamiliar. No matter how delightful Evelyn could be to those outside her family, there was simply no way her family could be expected to share in the fun. If her family appeared at the nursing home at the same time I came through, I walked right past and saved my visit with Evelyn for another time. I once expressed to her son how much I enjoyed his mother, but saying so was a mistake and only hurt him. He knew why I enjoyed her. It was because she was now somebody he didn't know.

Evelyn, like many Alzheimer's patients, had a zest for mischief. As she lost her faculty for language, she brightened when I sat beside her and confided in a mischievous tone: Let's steal the medicine cart. Let's dump our coffee on the houseplants.

It didn't matter what I said. What did matter was the tone of mischief. Mischief was a sure way to bring Evelyn out of the doldrums and provoke a smile and laugh.

Bob

Bob, who talked me out of becoming a lawyer and later urged me to build my house, eventually became a grumpy old man. He and his long-time friend Marv, also getting grumpier, had a falling out. They each started to think the other was stealing. Being a contentious sort, Bob wasn't going to stand by and allow his tools to be taken!

Bob's life began to fall apart in small ways. His wife Sharon broke her arm and rehabbed in the nursing home, enjoying her stay so much she did not want to come home. No wonder! Bob, who had always leaned heavily on Sharon to cook meals and keep house, was getting more difficult by the week.

With his wife gone, Bob was marooned in his huge house. The nursing home was just up the hill, so he visited her daily. He ate uptown at the cafe. When Bob's memory slipped, his sons arranged a housekeeper who came daily and made sure he took his heart medications. He could still tell stories from his years as a rambunctious defense lawyer, but he would tell the same story several times per visit.

My friend Roger, Bob's son, frequently drove 275 miles north to be with his dad and to assess the situation. It was deteriorating fast.

Roger, by now a budding gourmet cook, often invited me to eat supper with them. I enjoyed conversing with Bob, who was full of questions about the nursery. To make conversation during an October visit, I told him how the guys at the nursery were attempting to put new plastic on the greenhouses. I spiced the story a bit, emphasizing how there could be no wind whatsoever, or the massive sheets of plastic would lift people up and throw them. The vivid, admittedly exaggerated, picture of grown men being thrown around by a sheet of plastic made an impact on Bob.

A few weeks later, Roger called. His dad had been admitted to the hospital with pneumonia. Would I come over for supper?

When I arrived at the house, I learned Bob was also completely out of touch with reality and very angry. He was angry at his sons for putting him in the hospital, which he was convinced was a prison, and he was angry with the hospital staff for "illegally detaining him without informing him of the charges against him."

Just as we sat down to eat, the phone rang. The hospital staff was at their wits end; Bob was trying to climb out the third story window. Despite pneumonia, he was a strong eighty-five-year-old. Three staff members were trying to keep him from pulling off his escape. The message was clear. Either Roger hustled there within a half hour, or the staff would call the police.

With the hospital exactly thirty minutes away, we left dinner on the table and sped away.

When we got there, Bob was raging. The window was open. Three staff still wrestled with him. Now, he was furious at Roger. It was a grim scene.

I went along hoping Bob would recognize me and enter into one of our usual civil conversations.

He recognized me, all right, but now he expected me to help him get released from jail. I asked him to take a walk with me down the hall and was amazed when he agreed.

He was in no mood to talk.

"Hello, Bob!" a nurse chirped.

Bob flipped his middle finger.

"Have they ever held you in this place against your will?" he asked.

"Well," I said, "I was in here once for hernia surgery."

He grunted, unimpressed. He was still convinced this was a prison, not a hospital.

"If you want a strange feeling," I said, trying to get Bob's mind on a different topic by describing hernia symptoms, "try having your intestines press down against your testicles!"

"I didn't know you had any," he said, flipping off the next nurse right in her face.

He was in no mood for humor.

"Look here." I tried to interest him in an artistic landscape photograph on the wall. "These old trees are growing on the side of a roadbed. That means that road was built over a century ago. In fact, it most likely was originally a rail bed."

I was proud of my clever historic observation, and he sensed it. Having none of my photographic criticism, he looked right at me and in the caustic, contemptuous voice I imagined he used in the courtroom to destroy a witness, said slowly, "You really think you're hot shit, don't you?"

"Yes," I said, trying not to laugh, "I do."

Bob had been given sedatives, and they started to kick in. Roger discussed the situation with the ruffled staff while his dad and I walked back to his room. The window was shut and the temperature slowly warmed from the hour's worth of frigid November wind that had gusted through. Bob sat on the edge of his bed, still in a foul mood but losing energy fast.

Within minutes he fell asleep. He would be heavily sedated from now until his pneumonia subsided—or he expired, which most of us expected.

Bob got better, but he never went home again. The pneumonia seemed to accelerate the progress of his dementia. The diagnosis of Alzheimer's was immediate, and Bob was moved to a unit where he spent the last eleven months of his life. He seemed happy there, although as a man who loved to build arguments, he was clearly frustrated with his increased inability to put together a simple sentence.

Although Alzheimer's is said to knock out memories in reverse chronological order, Bob remembered one thing about me, even after he couldn't come up with my name: The story I told about the men putting on the greenhouse plastic. When I visited, he was agitated and worried looking until I assured him the plastic was securely on the greenhouses and would be good for the next four years.

"Good, good," he said, happy to have that settled. His eyes drifted shut like a cat starting a nap.

Marv

About the same time, Marv—with whom Bob cut firewood and shared machinery, yard work, and carpentry projects—was also diagnosed with early-onset Alzheimer's disease. A retired wrestling coach, he continued to lift weights even after his dementia took its toll.

Marv's descent to institutionalization was every bit as traumatic as Bob's. He was athletic enough to climb the walls in the courtyard at the first unit to take him. He was kicked out of two subsequent facilities that couldn't handle him, either. Finally, he calmed enough to stay in one place.

Bob and Marv, two very proud men, were felled—not in their prime—during a retirement that might have, without Alzheimer's disease, been long and rich. Both knew their lives were falling apart and raged against the decline. Sadly, people around Marv and Bob suffered—without support—the men's rage, confusion and sadness, as well as sadness of their own as the two men became strangers, sometimes even adversaries, to their own friends and kin.

Ken and Jill

I had no idea what good could happen after a dementia diagnosis until I met Ken, a giant of a man who had been diagnosed with Alzheimer's seven years earlier. He and his wife Jill now speak frequently on the topic of living with the disease.

Ken was a hard-driven professional. When he retired, he was at a loss. He had cultivated no hobbies. He was something of a social recluse. His job had been his life. His retirement was not entirely voluntary or welcome. Jill noticed Ken's personality had changed. Not sure if it was depression related to retirement, Jill talked Ken into seeing a doctor.

Ken and Jill had the rare experience of running into a perceptive general practitioner. He suggested Ken undergo a battery of cognitive tests, which revealed with a high certainty that Ken had Alzheimer's disease.

Some people argue that, because there is no cure, there is no need to diagnose the disease early and subject the sufferer to the additional pain of knowing recovery is hopeless. Indeed, after the diagnosis Ken and Jill both fell into a year of depression. They withdrew from what few social affairs they maintained. They hunkered down and waited for the end.

Then, another insightful and compassionate doctor intervened. Find a support group, he said. Go to classes. Fill up your social schedule. Make each day full. In other words, get busy, the doctor told them. Jill, in particular, took the advice to heart.

Although they had lived, worked, and retired in one of America's great cultural centers, Jill and Ken found it lacked resources for Alzheimer's patients. Despite having no relatives in Minnesota, they moved to Minneapolis, lured by the city's many programs for dementia sufferers. Never before had they even visited a cold climate, but they never regretted the move.

Ken and Jill filled their calendar. A breakfast club six days per week. Concerts. Lectures. Readings. Support groups. Visiting with other Alzheimer's sufferers. Speaking to groups. Ken's social life was ten times more active than before. Both he and Jill came to life.

When I heard them speak seven years after the diagnosis, the couple sparkled. The only outward indication Ken had any problem at all was when he stood next to me at the coffee machine. For a brief moment, I could tell he wondered where in the hell he was. He looked around for clues, figured it out, and was fine.

Heeding the doctor's suggestion, Ken and Jill took drastic action. They changed their life and their social habits completely. They moved to a distant and unfamiliar city. They made friends. And both said they considered the last few years, years they worked together in Alzheimer's education, the most rewarding of their marriage.

Did Ken and Jill's many activities slow the progress of his dementia? We'll never know. What is clear is the early diagnosis allowed Ken and Jill to not only make the best of a bad situation, but to enter a new chapter of life more fulfilling than any previous chapter.

Nun

A few years ago, I attended a leadership workshop held in a convent's retreat center. The theme? Live your dreams! Most of the registrants were idealistic sorts whose dreams involved grandiose projects like ending homelessness or world hunger.

After the early afternoon session, several of us stepped outside the front entrance for a breath of fresh air. I struck up a conversation with an earnest, young corporate employee who was at the workshop seeking the gumption to set up his own business.

Two elderly nuns lumbered up the sidewalk, one supporting the other. The more talkative sister was clearly in her late eighties, the supportive sister in her early seventies. Since I gravitate to older people, I turned from the young businessman to the nuns.

"Do you know what these are?" The older woman pointed toward some shrubs. Well, of course I know what they are, I said. I am a nurseryman!

"Why are they here?" she demanded. I made something up.

"You wouldn't make a very good teacher," she said, randomly, a clue that she had dementia. She was in a rollicking mood, a bit contentious, and not making complete sense.

"Were you a teacher?" I asked.

"Yes I was!" she answered, almost defiantly.

We joked and laughed, she accusing me of not being very good at this and that and I battling back.

Eventually, she pointed at a shrub that had lost its leaves. "That thing's going to grab us!"

Indeed, the gnarled shrub looked like it could reach out and nab any passer-by.

The younger nun smiled tightly, clearly uncomfortable with the exchange. Sadly, she hustled away the older woman who still babbled about bushes and teaching.

When I turned back to the businessman and the rest of the "Live Your Dreams" crowd, they were long gone.

Palma and Ella

Like many dementia victims, Palma and Ella were out of touch with what the rest of us consider to be reality, but were in perfect touch with each other. They jabbered in their own nonsensical way. They sat in the hall at Fair Meadow Nursing Home and commented on the passing scene. You could only guess what they were saying, which was probably fortunate.

When they tired, Palma and Ella fell asleep on each other's shoulder. It was a precious thing to watch, and the staff did what they could to nurture the friendship.

At naptime one afternoon, according to a nurse at the station, Ella suddenly lifted her head from Palma's shoulder and looked around, confused. She woke her companion.

"Where are we?" Ella asked.

Palma snorted, incredulous.

"You're asking *me*?"

That settled, the two went back to sleep.

Thelma

Each time I visited, Thelma signaled the nurses with her finger and mumbled incoherently. I wondered what was disturbing her—until I thought it through.

From the time Thelma married in her early twenties to the time she left the farm, when a visitor arrived, the first thing she did was offer coffee. A good farm wife, and Thelma had been the best, would never think of letting a guest sit down without at least starting the coffee.

Using this memory, I decided to try something: When Thelma started to signal the nurse and mumble, I said, "Oh, no, Thelma, I've had so much coffee I couldn't hold another sip. You just sit down and let's visit."

I used gestures to correspond with the words, emphatic gestures that, along with the tone of my voice, probably did more to get my point across than the content of the sentence.

Thelma would laugh and sit back and relax.

There is a soothing familiarity to small talk. In a rural town at harvest time, the talk is of harvest. During a blizzard, the talk is of the blizzard. By simply mimicking those poetic rhythms, I created a comfortable space for Thelma. Even if she didn't understand the verbiage, she comprehended the content.

So I talked about how the field work was going and how the men folks were working long hours, but how they'd have plenty of time in the winter to catch up on their sleep, so they'd better keep busy now!

"That's for sure," Thelma responded. "You just never know."

One time, I had my laptop. I showed Thelma some vacation pictures. She reacted with oohs and ahs. Then, I showed some pictures of Great Aunt Olive, who lived just down the hall. Although Thelma would never know Olive's name, she pointed at the screen and said, "I can just hear her!" The picture gave Thelma a chance to utter one of her simple phrases, a sort of competence phrase that allowed her to converse.

Another time, I brought a colorful garden catalog for Aunt Olive. As I passed Thelma in the dining hall, I paused and showed it to her, and she lit up.

"Oh, look there!" She pointed to the colorful pictures of flowers.

"You can keep this!" I said, congratulating myself for my spontaneous generosity.

I moved on down the hall. When I looked back at Thelma, she had set the catalog aside on a table, leaned her head against her hand, and appeared to be falling asleep. I realized that the fun of the colorful catalog for Thelma, at her current stage of dementia, was entirely in poring over it with me. Looking at the catalog alone meant little or nothing to her. The catalog's value was that it made it easier to connect with somebody and feel conversationally competent.

Grief

Art and Alma Kyllander

The nursery phone rang on a busy March morning. The woman on the other end was hysterical. It took me awhile to figure out it was Laura, the daughter-in-law of old neighbors Art and Alma. She had just found her seemingly healthy fifty-two-year-old husband Lynn dead on the kitchen floor of a heart attack.

"Could you just go sit with Lynn's parents?" Laura pled, concerned for their shock and grief. I was in the car in a minute, off to town where Art and Alma now lived in senior apartments.

Naturally, I worried what sort of scene I would find when I got there. They had just lost their only son and gotten the call only minutes before. I wasn't a minister. What role would I play?

I knocked on the door.

"Come in." Alma was right there with a hug, her eyes moist.

I clumsily mumbled, "My sympathies," and patted Art on the back, about the most affection allowed old-timers in Northern Minnesota.

"Yep," Art said. "That was a tough one."

He resumed his traditional pose at the kitchen table, hand planted firmly on the knob of his cane, eyes slowly opening and closing like those of a sleepy cat.

Alma, meanwhile, bustled off to get the coffee ready.

I pulled up a chair and didn't say much.

"Yes, you never know," Alma said, pouring the steaming coffee. "Cream?"

There was nothing more to be said, except to note that Lynn, who was as healthy and strong as a horse, had just lost a kidney to cancer, only to be felled by a heart attack three weeks after being declared cancer-free.

"You never know," Alma repeated.

After a long pause, Art said, "So, what's going on at the nursery?"

We were in the midst of early-season preparations, trying to pull pots and bags of soil from snow banks and melt them off so we could start potting and planting. The agonizing springs in Minnesota offer ample opportunities for comedy as trucks get stuck and tractors lose traction and snow banks collapse in the wrong direction. After a couple of sentences, I stopped, not knowing how much detail Art wanted to get into at this time of grief. Turns out, he wanted all kinds of detail. Alma chimed in with stories from her forty years working at the nursery, and soon we were off in memory land, talking about old times.

Art was nearly ninety; Alma was two years behind. They had lived next door to the nursery since before it was a nursery and they knew stories about my relatives I had never heard. I took a chance and nudged Art to tell a little about my great-grandfather Ole, who was a drunk. Soon, he was swaying his head back and forth, alternately squinting his eyes shut and opening them to make a point.

When he finished, Alma, who had a little tremor for as long

as I remembered, pursed her lips and trembled a bit more than usual, and I knew she was about to embark on a story. It took a while for her to get rolling, but once she did, the punch line came perfectly timed. Alma told about digging through the garbage next to Grandpa's desk at the nursery to pull out the checks that had come in the mail. Grandpa, it seems, was more interested in the correspondence than the money and frequently tossed the envelope in the garbage with the check still inside.

Their son Lynn's death earlier that morning wasn't mentioned again for an entire hour, which passed quickly. We had a great visit. As I got up to leave, I gave the usual benediction for such an occasion. "If you need anything, let me know."

"We sure will," Alma said. "Thanks for stopping."

Her face darkened. The fun moments were over and now she and Art were going to face their grief again.

Juanita

When neighbor Juanita lost her husband, she felt ashamed of her lack of shock and loss. Ken was a silent loner who spent most of his time out at the farm eight miles from their house in town.

After hugging a long line of mourners who seemed more upset than she, Juanita said with exasperation, "I'd be more sad, but he was never home!"

Great Aunt Olive

When her last sibling and youngest brother Burnett passed away peacefully at ninety-six, Aunt Olive mourned for a finite amount of time.

"I think I mourned Burnett yesterday morning," she said.

And then she was done with it.

Art Kyllander

I remember what old Art told me when I arrived immediately after the sudden death of his son. When I walked in, it couldn't have been more than an hour after he learned the news, yet Art used the past tense in describing his grief.

"Yep, that was a tough one."

I don't think Art's use of "was" was accidental. It was as if Art had dealt with the worst of the blow and was already working on moving forward. Indeed, Art lived to the ripe old age of ninety-seven and enjoyed most of his days.

112-Year-Old

I once read an interview of a 112-year-old woman who still possessed all her faculties and had a quality life. The interviewer wanted to find out her secret to longevity. However, the morning of the interview, the woman's daughter had died of natural causes at age eighty-six. The interviewer expected the interview to be canceled.

The mother would hear nothing of it. The interview would go on, she said, because the secret to living a long time was not to dwell on the negative.

My initial reaction was, good grief, lady, you could give yourself one day to recover. But no, she knew it was essential for her well-being to grieve briefly and then move on. She realized she had a golden opportunity to show others what it takes to live to such an advanced age.

Oscar

His voice trembled.

"Did you hear that my wife left me?" asked my neighbor, Oscar, the day his wife Inga died.

The two were inseparable and loving all of their sixty-five years together. Inga was ill for many of those years, and Oscar steadfastly took care of her without complaint. A gentleman to the core, he tended his yard, his farm, his garden, and any project he took on with the utmost in loving tenderness. He exhibited the same ethic when he tenderly cared for his wife through her years of depression.

After Inga was gone, Oscar began to fade. It wasn't long before he, too was gone.

Optometrist

The receptionist for an eye doctor in a neighboring town tells of a very elderly man who came to get his glasses adjusted. A few seconds after he left the lobby, he bounced back in, his demeanor stoic.

"Could you come and check on my wife? I think she might be dead."

The receptionist, also trained as a nurse, ran to the car. The wife was indeed dead. The receptionist knew enough not to call the paramedics, aware the ambulance crew, bless their hearts, was legally obligated to hook the dead woman to electrodes and try to start her up again.

Her advice to the old man?

"Let's just drive over to the funeral home and drop her off there."

They did and, despite the sadness of the occasion, preserved a dignity and quietude often absent at death.

Marguerite

Marguerite cared for her cancer-riddled husband for five years before he passed away. Although she looked worn and haggard at the funeral, almost as if she was ready to jump in the grave behind her husband, Marguerite soon began to flourish. She wore flowing scarves and capes and became involved with volunteer work of every sort. When she contracted cancer herself at age eighty-eight, she announced she was not treating it. She had learned her lesson by watching her husband linger for years. Instead, Marguerite would take painkillers and enjoy life until the last possible moment.

When I heard they called in hospice for Marguerite, I assumed she had only days to live. That same afternoon, I saw her at the coffee shop, bedecked in scarves and a fashionable hat. I gawked.

"What's the matter with you?" Marguerite asked.

"I thought you were in hospice," I said.

"Oh, they only come Tuesdays and Thursdays," she replied with a dismissive wave of her hand.

Last Visits

89-Year-Old

A hospice nurse was granted an opportunity she couldn't turn down: A six-week training session in Washington, D. C. Sadly, however, that meant she had to say goodbye to her present roster of patients—including a gentleman to whom she had grown attached; he might die in a couple of weeks, if not within days.

The day before she left, the nurse visited her patient. She dreaded saying goodbye. She didn't want to leave the dying man before her job was done. Tearfully, she bid him farewell, saying she'd see him in some future place.

Her patient was kind and returned her hugs, but after she left, he turned to his wife and asked, "Just where in the hell does she think I'm going?"

Great Aunt Olive

Great Aunt Olive has a knack for ending up in the right place at the right time when it comes to "the last visit."

"We need to go see Uncle Johnny. Now."

Even over the phone, I heard the uncharacteristic urgency in her voice. Her brother Johnny had suffered a stroke and was in a coma.

I dropped everything and drove, in dirty work clothes, twenty miles to her place, picked her up, then drove another forty to the hospital where we joined the family in the intensive care unit. Johnny's blood pressure was down to nearly nothing. Aunt Olive held his hand as he slipped away.

She had a soft spot for Johnny that never hardened. Even at eighty-five-years-old, he was still her baby brother.

Great Aunt Gertrude

Another time, Great Aunt Olive pressed me to go see her oldest sister Gertrude who was in her mid-nineties. She was nice enough, but all I really remembered about her was her perpetual scowl and the enormous box sunglasses she wore even indoors. It was a bit odd for Aunt Olive to press me to visit because Aunt Gertrude had been anything but convivial with her over the years, criticizing her bitterly for Aunt Olive's wandering ways and inability to keep money in her purse.

I ignored Aunt Olive's plea. The next time she brought it up, however, it was more a demand. You need to go visit Aunt Gertrude. She has stories to tell that you need to hear.

So, I did. Aunt Gertrude lived in a sparsely furnished room at the retirement center. She had moved there recently and seemed not to want to decorate her room with any signs of permanence. She wanted nothing to do with the place.

Aunt Gertrude was glad to see me and seemed to have been expecting me. I don't know if Aunt Olive called to tell her I was coming. I doubt it. Either way, it seemed Aunt Gertrude knew my mission was to hear her tell her stories before she died.

She obliged.

She told story after story. Of her marriage. Of her struggle the first years of their marriage. Of their poverty. Of her illnesses as a young mother. And finally, about her beloved son Dale, who had joined the military and finished basic training near Memphis, Tennessee. He and his buddies decided to go see a minor league baseball game.

Aunt Gertrude described the game. And in a moment I'll never forget, she pointed her bony finger at me and said in a raised voice, "And the Chicks won!

"And then on the way home...."

Aunt Gertrude shrugged and looked at her lap. I knew what had happened. Her son's car crashed and he burned to death.

After two hours, I left, full of family lore.

Aunt Gertrude died a few weeks later. And Aunt Olive asked me, "Weren't you glad you got to hear Gertrude's story?"

I was.

Great Aunt Norma

Uncle Johnny's widow Norma, always a picture of health and busyness, developed bone cancer. For a couple of years she carried on as if nothing was eating away at her body, but finally, or so we were told, the cancer had progressed to the point where Norma's days were numbered. The doctors sent Norma home and stopped treatments.

At that point, Great Aunt Olive called. "We need to go see Norma."

I dreaded the visit. It was obvious this would be our last and I could only imagine the morbidity and emotion it would involve.

However, when Aunt Olive and I walked in we found Norma looking just a little weaker than normal, her hair in good shape, as always, and snacks on the table, as always. Not a word was said about her condition or her illness, except for a passing, "Well, we'll see how this works out first."

Norma, we had been warned, was exhausted and could only sustain a visit of ten minutes or so.

Not on this day. Norma started to tell stories. The two women rocked with laughter. She told about the time the cat dug into the pie as it cooled on the porch while the ladies from the mission circle were waiting to eat it in the next room. She told about the time she sent hapless Johnny to the wrong funeral, only to realize her error after he left—and how she waited to torment him when he got home.

"They kept pronouncing his name wrong," Johnny said, having no idea he was at the wrong church.

"So, how'd he look?" Norma replied, barely concealing her glee.

"Oh, they all look the same," Johnny said with a shrug.

Norma talked about her first husband, the first I'd ever heard him mentioned. He drank, she said. He was killed in a construction accident. Even with three small children to rear, Norma swore she would never have anything to do with men again.

While working as a waitress to support her family, Norma met Johnny. She described how he let only her wait on him and gradually worked up the courage to give her a lift home in a pouring rainstorm. How kind Johnny was to her children. How glad she was he didn't drink. How her children loved Johnny. All of this was history I had never heard.

Then Norma talked about how life on the farm wasn't easy for women. How bachelors arrived to mooch free food at suppertime. Every night. Gjelmer, she found out, couldn't stand macaroni and

cheese. So, she made up an enormous vat of the stuff and stored it in the refrigerator. When Gjelmer's car appeared in the driveway, supper was whisked away and Norma heated up the macaroni and cheese. Twice she fed him the despised dish and that bachelor never again showed up at mealtime.

We laughed and laughed and stayed until Aunt Olive and I got tired—although Norma still seemed fresh. As we left, we said nothing about the "last visit." Instead, we talked about how much fun we had. We didn't say anything about doing it again; we knew we probably wouldn't. It was a joyful farewell.

Norma died three weeks later. She entered the nursing home in her final days and told an aide matter-of-factly the morning of her death, "I am going to die today, you know."

When Aunt Olive and I recalled Norma's death, all Aunt Olive could talk about was what fun we had on our last visit.

Endings

87-Year-Old

A couple of years back, I joined a group of community members to tour an assisted living facility in a neighboring town in preparation for designing one of our own. Our committee was particularly impressed by the memory care unit. I asked one of the residents in the unit what he thought of the place.

He loved it there, he said. Enjoyed every day. Great food. Good company. Lots of windows.

"Business is booming!" he said, optimistically.

I asked him what sort of business he was in, expecting a demented and possibly enjoyable trip into the past.

"Dying," the man said cheerfully. "That's what we do around here. And it's not a bad place to die."

Grandpa Melvin

I was in sixth grade when Grandpa had his first heart attack. It was a dark December evening. Grandma called on the intercom from their house across the yard, "Grandpa's sick!" The tone in her voice and the immediate click of the phone meant it was serious.

It was 1976, just before small towns in Minnesota began to train their own Emergency Medical Technicians and improve their ambulance services dramatically. The ambulance didn't arrive for an hour. When it did, the driver was alone and had no medical expertise. He was a transporter, nothing more.

Children were not a part of life-and-death emergencies in that era. Dad raced to my grandpa and grandma's house and dealt with the possible tragedy on his own while Mom stayed with us three children. We opened the window to hear what was going on, even though it was below freezing. We were scared. The terror? Grandpa might die. Nothing of the sort had happened to our family before.

Fifteen years later, I stood in Grandpa and Grandma's nursing home room along with nursing home staff and three paramedics when Grandpa actually did pass away at age eighty-six. To my surprise, the event was completely natural. Grandpa made it through his death with minimal trauma. His heart simply—stopped. I managed to witness it, a possibility I had dreaded for decades.

It happened, and we all made it through. For the first time, I understood death is natural. In fact, it is the most natural thing on earth.

Art Kyllander

Old neighbor Art Kyllander (the same man I visited, along with his wife Alma, when their son passed away unexpectedly) was ninety-seven years old and fading a bit. He had played whist on Tuesday, but by Thursday, his doctor decided he had better be placed in the nursing home.

Two days later, I stopped in. The nurse at the desk told me he wasn't doing very well. She was right. In fact, as I walked down the hall, I could see by the grieving relatives that Art was not long for this world. I was tempted to turn and hightail it out the front door. Part of me didn't want to intrude upon the private moment with his family; another part hoped to avoid the trauma of a deathbed scene.

But before I could leave, Alma caught sight of me. I walked into the room and gave her a hug. She was in tears.

"It's tough," she said. She and her husband had spent over seventy-five years together.

Art heaved for breath.

"Eric is here to see you!" Alma hollered right over Art's face, before I could make my exit.

Art grunted.

Alma gestured for me to take her place and say hi. I did. He opened his eyes for a second.

"Good to see you," Art rasped, barely audible.

I got the feeling that if he had the energy, he would have passed some comment on the weather. I backed from the bed, said goodbye to Alma and her daughter, and drove home.

As I walked in the door, the phone rang.

"We wanted you to know that Art just died."

I hung up the phone, honored beyond description.

Alma and her daughter had summoned me to join them in Art's final moments. To make their generosity complete, I was one of the first they called after his heart stopped beating.

Great Aunt Olive

Phone calls at 4:30 a.m. are spooky, especially when you have an elderly relative in the nursing home. And indeed, this phone call was from the nursing home—regarding then ninety-eight-year-old Aunt Olive—but the nurse's tone was oddly jovial.

"We found Olive on the floor—not breathing, unresponsive—at three o'clock this morning," she said.

That didn't sound good.

"A staff member administered CPR until the EMTs arrived," she went on, "and they took her up to the hospital."

All right, is that all?

"I want you to know Olive regained consciousness just as she was being strapped to the gurney," the nurse continued. "When we informed her that she needed to go to the hospital, she got very upset."

Why was that, I asked.

"'I am going *nowhere* without my eyebrow pencil!' she told us."

So, before they could roll Aunt Olive down the hall to the ambulance, an aide found her pencil and drew on some eyebrows.

By the next afternoon, she was home at Fair Meadow as if nothing had happened.

For Aunt Olive, looking good is not optional, even when you think you're staring death in the face!

My Purpose

Eric

After two hours of lonely driving, it was a relief to arrive at the busiest establishment in the quiet town of Hallock, Minnesota—the nursing home. Over one hundred people—most of them very old, some fully aware, others not—gathered in the community room to listen and watch me entertain.

A woman in a reclining wheelchair at the back of the room stared blankly at the ceiling, mouth agape. I moved closer to make eye contact and greet her, but received no response. Even so, I positioned myself within range of her gaze, hoping she was somewhere behind that vacant face.

I performed my song and dance. I pounded the piano in rousing ragtime. I crooned old country songs. I told funny stories. All the while, I wondered if the woman stretched out at the back of the room absorbed any of it.

I wanted to talk to her again, but after I finished, a little line formed. Two old men told me their favorite Ole and Lena jokes. Others chatted about mutual connections in my hometown. Meanwhile, staff rolled the woman back to her room.

In the background lingered a dignified, white-haired gentleman sporting a bright red cardigan. After the room emptied, he stepped forward to shake hands. He had rarely been to Minnesota, he told me, until seven years ago when his wife suffered a stroke that left her unable to speak or walk.

So he—who had never lived in a small town—moved from California to a hamlet on the remote, windswept prairies of Minnesota, his wife's home state. Small towns in this state have caring nursing homes, he had heard, and he heard right. He bought a house in Hallock. His wife had been cared for very well. He visited her every day.

She was the very resident who'd snagged my eye.

"Since her stroke," he said, "my wife has shown few indications that she is aware of much. But tonight? When you imitated George Jones?"

His voice quivered.

"Tonight—I saw her smile."

To order additional copies of this book
or other books by Eric Bergeson

visit
www.countryscribe.com

or email the author at ericberg@gvtel.com

or write to
Country Scribe Publishing
4177 County Highway 1
Fertile, MN 56540